Please remember that this is a library book,
and that it belongs only temporarily to each
person who uses it. Be considerate. Do
not write in this, or any, library book.

WITHDRAWN

WITHDRAWN

Other People's Children

Other People's Children

Cultural Conflict in the Classroom

Lisa Delpit

The New Press · New York

PUBLISHED IN THE UNITED STATES BY THE NEW PRESS, NEW YORK
DISTRIBUTED BY W.W. NORTON & COMPANY, INC.,
500 FIFTH AVENUE, NEW YORK, NY 10110

"Skills and Other Dilemmas of a Progressive Black Educator" first appeared in *Harvard Educational Review*, 56:4, pp. 379–385. Copyright © 1986 by the President and Fellows of Harvard College. All rights reserved.

"The Silenced Dialogue: Power and Pedagogy in Educating Other People's Children" first appeared in *Harvard Educational Review*, 58:3, pp. 280–298. Copyright © 1988 by the President and Fellows of Harvard College. All rights reserved.

"Language Diversity and Learning" first appeared in *Perspectives on Talk and Learning*, Susan Hynds and Donald L. Rubin, eds. Copyright © 1990 by the National Council of Teachers of English. Reprinted with permission.

"The Politics of Teaching Literate Discourse" first appeared in *Freedom's Plow*, Theresa Perry and James Fraser, eds. Copyright © 1993 by Routledge. Reprinted with permission.

ISBN 1–56584–179–4
LC 94–069571

ESTABLISHED IN 1990 AS A MAJOR ALTERNATIVE TO THE LARGE, COMMERCIAL PUBLISHING HOUSES, THE NEW PRESS IS THE FIRST FULL-SCALE NONPROFIT AMERICAN BOOK PUBLISHER OUTSIDE OF THE UNIVERSITY PRESSES. THE PRESS IS OPERATED EDITORIALLY IN THE PUBLIC INTEREST, RATHER THAN FOR PRIVATE GAIN; IT IS COMMITTED TO PUBLISHING IN INNOVATIVE WAYS WORKS OF EDUCATIONAL, CULTURAL, AND COMMUNITY VALUE THAT, DESPITE THEIR INTELLECTUAL MERITS, MIGHT NOT NORMALLY BE "COMMERCIALLY" VIABLE. THE NEW PRESS'S EDITORIAL OFFICES ARE LOCATED AT THE CITY UNIVERSITY OF NEW YORK.

BOOK DESIGN BY CHARLES NIX

PRODUCTION MANAGEMENT BY KIM WAYMER

PRINTED IN THE UNITED STATES OF AMERICA

95 96 97   9 8 7 6 5 4 3 2

For Maya, Colin and Qasim —

While you are with us,
you belong not to us,
For your souls dwell in a
place of tomorrow
Which we cannot visit,
not even in our dreams.

(INFLUENCED BY KAHLIL GIBRAN'S *The Prophet*)

Contents

Acknowledgments

Writing a first book can never be easy, but when the writing is coupled with working full time and being the single mother of a five-year-old, it could be impossible without the support and encouragement of friends, family members, and colleagues. I owe thanks to many.

I would never have discovered that I had something worth saying if not for Badi Foster, Ken Haskins, Chet Pierce, and Courtney Cazden – four very special people who were my professors at Harvard's Graduate School of Education. They taught not only with their lectures but with their lives.

This volume would not exist were it not for two dear friends. Herb Kohl pushed and prodded me to write – even getting editors to call *me* when I was less than enthusiastic about the prospect. Alma Roberts was there throughout the book's gestation and birth with words of encouragement and numerous offers for quality childcare.

My former boss, Dr. Robert Hill, and the rest of the staff at Morgan State University's Institute for Urban Research always made work a pleasure. From the time I returned to my job as new mother and found a playpen in my office until the day I sadly said good-bye, they supported all of my work efforts. I must particularly thank my research assistant, Sharon Futrell. Sharon not only kept my life in order but typed copy after copy of the manuscript without a sign of complaint.

My wonderful family has been and continues to be an

unending source of inspiration, knowledge, and support. They instilled in me the ethic of concern for others and taught me to live with care upon this earth. In order to ensure that I would have the time and space to write without distraction, my sister and her husband, Billie and Clarence "Skee" Cunningham, generously allowed me the use of their isolated beach house while my mother, Mrs. Edmae Butler, loved and nurtured my rambunctious daughter for three weeks. (And thanks, Billie and Skee, for bringing Maya to visit me when neither of us could go another day without a mother-daughter hug.) Kevin, Helena, Joe, Precious, Deedy, Desi – all of you helped make this book possible.

Special love and thanks must go to my Maya, who keeps me working to create a better future. She gave up big chunks of mommy-time so that I could write. (Yes, sweetie, when you grow up you can help me write another book.)

I owe much to my editors at the New Press. Diane Wachtell made me believe I could do this. She and Ellen Reeves provided the utmost in quality, patient editorial assistance, while at the same time supplying an abundance of warmth and friendship. They have enriched my life, professionally and personally. I am fortunate to have gotten to know them.

Finally, I thank the children, parents, and teachers who have shared so much of their lives with me. Individuals in the far corners of the planet have taught critical lessons about "other people's children" and patiently guided my learning. I owe them all a debt I can never repay.

Introduction

SCENE I

Carolyn is a young Irish-American kindergarten teacher who has been teaching for five years. The school at which she has taught has been a predominantly white, middle-class school in a quiet neighborhood in New England. However, because of recent redistricting, the school population now includes children from a housing project not far away. These children are almost exclusively poor and black. Thus, Carolyn and the other teachers in the school are newly faced with a population of children with whom they are completely unfamiliar.

I am working on a research project with Carolyn. She has asked me to observe a little boy named Anthony, a five-year-old black child from "the projects," whom she has defined as a child with behavioral, learning, and language problems. She wants to use the results of my observations to "get him help."

In my observations of Anthony in the classroom, I have noticed that he gets almost no positive feedback during the course of a day, and instead receives a tremendous number of negative comments. I have taken Anthony out into the hallway several times to talk and play privately so as to get a better assessment of his actual abilities. The following dialogue is taken from a transcript of my conference with Carolyn about my observations. I am attempting to point out some of Anthony's positive points to Carolyn:

L: Anthony told me that he liked school and that his favorite thing in his class was group time.

C: That's amazing, since he can't sit still in it. He just says anything sometimes. In the morning he's OK; after nap he's impossible.

* * *

L: He's really talking more, it seems!

C: He's probably never allowed to talk at home. He needs communicative experience. I was thinking of referring him to a speech therapist. He probably never even got to use scissors at home.

* * *

L: He told me about his cousin he plays with after school. It seems he really does have things to talk about.

C: It's unfortunate, but I don't think he even knows what family means. Some of these kids don't know who their cousins are and who their brothers and sisters are.

Scene II

Charles is a three-year-old African-American boy who likes a little white girl in my daughter's nursery school class. Like most three-year-olds, his affection is expressed as much with hugs as with hits. One morning I notice that Charles has been hovering around Kelly, his special friend. He grabs her from behind and tries to give her a bear hug. When she protests, the teacher tells him to stop. A short time later he returns to her table to try to kiss her on the cheek. She protests again and the teacher puts him in "time-out." I comment to the teacher with a smile that Charles certainly seems to have a little crush on Kelly. She frowns and replies that his behavior is "way out of line." She continues with disgust in her voice, "Sometimes what he does just looks like lust."

SCENE III

One evening I receive a telephone call from Terrence's mother, who is near tears. A single parent, she has struggled to put her academically talented fourteen-year-old African-American son in a predominantly white private school. As an involved parent, she has spoken to each of his teachers several times during the first few months of school, all of whom assured her that Terrence was doing "just fine." When the first quarter's report cards were issued, she observed with dismay a report filled with Cs and Ds. She immediately went to talk to his teachers. When asked how they could have said he was doing fine when his grades were so low, each of them gave her some version of the same answer: "Why are you so upset? For him, Cs are great. You shouldn't try to push him so much."

As I lived through each of these scenarios, a familiar sense of dread closed in around me: my throat constricted, my eyes burned, I found it hard to breathe. I have faced this fog too many times in my career in education. It is a deadly fog formed when the cold mist of bias and ignorance meets the warm vital reality of children of color in many of our schools. It is the result of coming face-to-face with the teachers, the psychologists, the school administrators who look at "other people's children" and see damaged and dangerous caricatures of the vulnerable and impressionable beings before them.

But we cannot blame the schools alone. We live in a society that nurtures and maintains stereotypes: we are all bombarded daily, for instance, with the portrayal of the young black male as monster. When we see a group of young black men, we lock our car doors, cross to the other side of the street, or clutch our handbags. We are constantly told of the one out of four black men who is involved with the prison system – but what about the three out of four who are not? During a major storm this past winter, a group of young black men in my neighborhood spent the day freeing cars that were stuck in the ice. When do we see their lives portrayed on the six o'clock news?

So, as a result of living in this society, their teachers make big assumptions about Anthony, Charles, and Terrence. They judge their actions, words, intellects, families, and communities as inadequate at best, as collections of pathologies at worst. These stories can be justifiably interpreted as examples of racism. However valid that interpretation may be, it is insufficient, for it gives us no clue as to how to resolve the problem. Indeed, these views are not limited to white adults. In my experience in predominantly black school districts, the middle-class African-American teachers who do not identify with the poor African-American students they teach may hold similarly damaging stereotypes. These adults probably are not bad people. They do not wish to damage children; indeed, they likely see themselves as wanting to help. Yet they are totally unable to perceive those different from themselves except through their own culturally clouded vision. In my experience, they are not alone.

We all carry worlds in our heads, and those worlds are decidedly different. We educators set out to teach, but how can we reach the worlds of others when we don't even know they exist? Indeed, many of us don't even realize that our own worlds exist only in our heads and in the cultural institutions we have built to support them. It is as if we are in the middle of a great computer-generated virtual reality game, but the "realities" displayed in various participants' minds are entirely different terrains. When one player moves right and up a hill, the other player perceives him as moving left and into a river.

What are we really doing to better educate poor children and children of color? Sporadically we hear of "minorities" scoring higher in basic skills, but on the same newspaper page we're informed of their dismal showing in higher-order thinking skills. We hear of the occasional school exemplifying urban excellence, but we are inundated with stories of inner-city mass failure, student violence, and soaring drop-out rates. We are heartened by new attempts at school improvement – better teacher education, higher standards, revised curricula – even while teachers of color are disappearing from the workforce and fiscal cutbacks increase class sizes, decimate critical instructional programs, and make it impossible to repair the buildings that are literally falling down around our children's heads.

What should we be doing? The answers, I believe, lie not in a proliferation of new reform programs but in some basic understandings of who we are and how we are connected to and disconnected from one another. I have come to some of those understandings through my own attempts to understand my place in this country as an African-American woman: I am the offspring of a teacher in a colored high school in pre-integration Louisiana and a man who received his GED diploma in his fortieth year, only to die of kidney failure at the age of forty-seven because the "colored ward" was not permitted to use the dialysis machine. I am the frightened teenager who was part of the first wave of black students to integrate hostile white high schools. I am the college student of the 1970s whose political and ethical perspectives were developed against the backdrop of the struggle for black liberation and the war in Vietnam. I am the panicked mother of a five-year-old soon to enter an urban public school system where I can no longer buffer her from damaging perspectives. I am the teacher of many diverse students – from African-American toddlers to Papua New Guinean preschoolers, and from Hispanic middle-schoolers to European-American college students, to Native Alaskan teachers.

The essays included in this book chronicle my journey into understanding other worlds, journeys that involved learning to see, albeit dimly, through the haze of my own cultural lenses. In that blurred view, I have come to understand that power plays a critical role in our society and in our educational system. The worldviews of those with privileged positions are taken as the only reality, while the worldviews of those less powerful are dismissed as inconsequential. Indeed, in the educational institutions of this country, the possibilities for poor people and for people of color to define themselves, to determine the self each should be, involve a power that lies outside of the self. It is others who determine how they should act, how they are to be judged. When one "we" gets to determine standards for all "wes," then some "wes" are in trouble!

*

The book is divided into three parts. The first contains two articles originally published in the *Harvard Educational Review* which stirred a great deal of controversy because they challenged aspects of popular approaches to literacy. "Process writing" and "whole language" advocates believed me to be attacking their "progressive" and "child-centered" methods of instruction, while I saw myself as struggling to figure out why some children of color in classrooms utilizing these methodologies were not learning to read and write, not acquiring the "codes of power" necessary for success in this society. These articles also questioned why teachers and parents of color were so seldom included in the conversations about what was good for their children. The third essay in Part 1 describes another aspect of my thinking, one that has seldom been considered in critiques of my work: even while teachers provide access to the "codes of power" represented by acquiring facility in "standard edited English," they must also value and make use in the classroom of the language and culture children bring from home.

Part 2 tries to find the origins of some of these views in my experiences and research, particularly through my work in Papua New Guinea and Alaska, where I learned to see the world through the eyes of those with very different histories. It was in those two settings that I first understood the need to step outside of myself and my beliefs in order to allow the perspectives of others to filter in. This part also includes a description of the results of research on the views and attitudes of teachers of color about their teacher education and subsequent teaching careers. With the number of students of color increasing in our public school systems every year, even as the number of teachers of color drops, I believe it is essential that we go directly to these seldom-asked teachers to identify the problems associated with their entering and remaining in the teaching profession.

Part 3 offers some thoughts on solutions and directions for our future as educators. I am not immodest enough to believe that I have the answers to the myriad problems facing education, but I do hope that these essays suggest some avenues for those working to find solutions. One piece is directed specifically to teachers on teaching literacy to disenfranchised students. Another presents recommendations to policy makers for making the assessment of teachers more sensitive to issues of cultural difference. The last part concludes with a more general essay on multicultural education, given as the Charles H. Thompson Lecture at Howard University, which I hope will interest people concerned with the improvement of education for those least well served by the public education system in this country.

Other People's Children

Part 1

Controversies Revisited

Controversies Revisited

The essays in this section were written for a variety of purposes. Taken together, they reflect my beliefs about educating children of color, particularly African-American children, in what for them are often alienating environments. The first two were written while I was in the throes of struggling to adapt to an alien environment myself – at the University of Alaska, Fairbanks (UAF), where I was involved in teacher training. It was there that I first found myself in a completely white professional setting. Although there were a few students of color, Native Alaskan and African-American, I was the only African-American woman faculty member at any of the three campuses of the University of Alaska. I was confused by the positions articulated by many of my colleagues, and I found them far removed from my own beliefs about education.

On one side there were the conservative traditionalists. These faculty members were often most critical of students who were not a part of the mainstream, and they frequently questioned these students' capacity to become teachers. If asked to define their own role, these academicians would likely define themselves as the upholders of traditional academic standards. One of these faculty members told a group of Native Alaskan students who wanted the university to provide a more culturally relevant education that it was not the purpose of UAF to serve the needs of Natives – so if they were interested in that kind of education, they had better start their own university.

On the other side were the anthropologically oriented liberals. These faculty members, who identified strongly with the Native

Alaskan students, saw their role as creating more opportunities for Native Alaskans to become certified to teach in their own village communities. Although I certainly felt more at home with the politics of these colleagues, I was troubled that, in their attempt to celebrate Native culture, many of them believed it unnecessary – even damaging – to teach Native students the skills they would need to survive in the larger society.

One Native student complained to me that some of these faculty members were teaching Natives only about Native culture – the only topic in which the professors thought they needed to be schooled in order to teach in Native villages. She felt that she and her fellow Native students were not learning how to teach math, reading, or science. How could village kids compete if their teachers didn't know how to teach academic subject matter? And, she continued, what about Native teachers who chose not to teach in villages but in town, where their students would be children of all ethnicities? What were they learning that would help them become truly competent teachers in any setting?

I also had doubts about what we as a faculty, visitors as we were to the region, knew about teaching people to teach in their own communities. I felt I had been educated away from how best to teach in my own community by well-meaning liberals, and I saw the university as possibly replicating that injustice.

Finding myself at odds with colleagues of both persuasions, I was further perturbed by what I saw happening to children of color and teachers of color in the Fairbanks schools. Just like the parents, teachers and children of color in East Coast cities I visited for conferences, Native Alaskans had little voice in determining what should happen to their children. White conservatives and liberals were battling each other over what was good for these "other people's children," while excluding from the conversation those with the most to gain or lose by its outcome.

This drama, though played out in many educational arenas, was often enacted in enclaves of teachers who embraced a new instructional methodology – namely, writing process approaches to literacy, sparked by the work of Donald Graves and others in New England. Because of my position as a literacy instructor at the university, I was well aware of the approach, and knew many of its proponents. The "process approach" proposed in part that teachers should focus more on the larger cognitive processes of writing than solely on correcting the products. Inspired by writings of Graves and others, groups of teachers all over the country developed grass-roots organizations to advance the concept. By the time these essays were written, there were many city or state "writing projects" in which teachers took major roles in sharing their expertise with other teachers, and a national organization had been founded.

I wrote "Skills and Other Dilemmas of a Progressive Black Educator" initially as a letter to a University of Alaska faculty colleague to lay out my concerns with the writing project movement and to detail the frustrations many teachers of color felt at being excluded from educational dialogue – in this case, the dialogue about literacy instruction.

When that short piece was later published as an article in the Harvard Educational Review *in 1986, I was unprepared for the intense interest and controversy it generated. Writing project members across the country were incensed. Despite my attempts to say that we must not abandon the very good ideas of the process approach, but must be open to modification based on the voices of parents and educators of color, they perceived me as unequivocally attacking their work. Many African-Americans, on the other hand, told me I had made public beliefs they thought no one else shared. I received letters from all over the country. African-American teachers thanked me for writing about their experience, and some white teachers wrote that the article helped them identify problems in their own classrooms; yet many questioned my motivation in attacking a well-meaning program that had the best interests of all children at heart.*

As a result of the controversy, I was asked to give a keynote speech at the University of Pennsylvania's Ethnography Conference in 1987. The second article in this part, "The Silenced Dialogue: Power and Pedagogy in Educating Other People's Children," is a version of that speech. That it would stir even more controversy than its predecessor might have been foreseen by the reaction of the audience to the speech. Amidst an undercurrent of whispered disapproval, one white woman rose to say that

*I was lying to suggest that black teachers weren't happy: I was
just trying to stir up trouble where none existed. Several of the
African-American teachers in the audience loudly and passionately challenged her position. When the session was ended due to
scheduling constraints, the passion continued. I found the
woman who had challenged me sobbing in the bathroom, sur-
rounded by a group of consoling white women. According to professors I encounter at national conferences who use the article in
their classes, student response is often as volatile.*

*These two articles, often considered a set, are among the
twenty articles that have received the most requests for reprints
in the history of the* Harvard Educational Review. *Even
though they were published in 1986 and 1988, the controver-
sies surrounding them continue. In a conversation on a computer
network brought to my attention by a graduate student, one
renowned white liberal literacy expert recently accused me of
joining the educational far right with what he perceived as my
critiques of his educational agenda. Other computer conversations have included defenses of my position by some white scholars, particularly those with a great deal of experience in
communities of color, and by African-American graduate students who seem to find it liberating to see in print positions they
held prior to graduate school but for which they found little or
no support from most of their professors.*

*Most gratifying to me have been those letters from teachers,
white* and *black, who have struggled to find more effective ways
to teach children of color but discovered current popular education practices to be inadequate. When they questioned the efficacy of the new programs in university classrooms, in in-service
sessions, or in the teacher's lounge, they found their voices
silenced. One African-American teacher, Opal Davis Dawson,
wrote that in her university class she was able to use some of the
words in the article to force her white colleagues into a conversation about culture that they had formerly refused to hold. She
wrote,*

> As you said in your article, they always feel they know what's
> best for everyone. Well I must say I put something on their
> minds. For an entire semester, they had snubbed me and

thought they were the ultimate. I must admit not many
spoke to me after that night, but then they never really spoke
before. As for my grade, I received an A! I felt that you
needed to know that story because you were my inspiration.

*Another graduate student at the time, Margaret McCasland,
wrote several very thought-provoking letters that were representative of other letters from white teachers. She detailed her
plight as a white student from a low-income family who also
had a worldview inconsistent with her university's take on
what is the best instruction for poor students. She found these
articles supported her efforts to clarify her positions and make
them known.*

*At first reading, these two articles may appear at odds with
the ideas expressed in the third piece in this section, "Language
Diversity and Learning," which was originally published in
1990 in a National Council of Teachers of English volume that
focused on language in the classroom. Explicitly stated in both
earlier articles is the caveat that neither position — neither skills
nor process, liberal nor conservative — is sufficient in and of itself,
yet many educators insist on dichotomizing my ideas, making me
a proponent or a detractor of one or another perspective.*

*I include this third article here to make explicit the balance I
actually advocate. I do not demand, as one white academic said,
that children of color give up what they are to become something
else. Nor do I, as he continued, "reject the concept that liberation
for poor kids and linguistic minorities starts with accepting
their culture and language and helping them to build on it."
Indeed, that is what I do advocate.*

Skills and Other Dilemmas of a Progressive Black Educator

Why do the refrains of progressive educational movements seem lacking in the diverse harmonies, the variegated rhythms, and the shades of tone expected in a truly heterogeneous chorus? Why do we hear so little representation from the multicultural voices which comprise the present-day American educational scene?

These questions have surfaced anew as I begin my third year of university "professoring" after having graduated from a prestigious university known for its progressive school of education. My family back in Louisiana is very proud about all of that, but still they find me rather tedious. They say things like, "She just got here and she's locked up in that room with a bunch of papers talking about she's gotta finish some article. I don't know why she bothers to come home." Or, "I didn't ask you about what any research said, what do *you* think?!"

I once shared my family's skepticism of academia. I remember asking myself in the first few months of my graduate school career, "Why is it these theories never seem to be talking about me?" But by graduation time many of my fellow minority students and I had become well trained: we had learned alternate ways of viewing the world, coaxed memories of life in our communities into forms which fit into the categories created by academic researchers and theoreticians, and internalized belief systems that often belied our own experiences.

I learned a lot in graduate school. For one thing I learned that people acquire a new dialect most effectively through interaction with speakers of that dialect, not through being constantly corrected. Of course, when I was growing up, my mother and my teachers in the pre-integration, poor black Catholic school that I attended corrected every other word I uttered in their effort to coerce my Black English into some-times hypercorrect Standard English forms acceptable to black nuns in Catholic schools. Yet, I learned to speak and write in Standard English.

I also learned in graduate school that people learn to write not by being taught "skills" and grammar, but by "writing in meaningful contexts." In elementary school I diagrammed thousands of sentences, filled in tens of thousands of blanks, and never wrote any text longer than two sentences until I was in the tenth grade of high school. I have been told by my pro-fessors that I am a good writer. (One, when told about my poor community and segregated, skill-based schooling, even went so far as to say, "How did you *ever* learn how to write?") By that time I had begun to wonder myself. Never mind that I had learned – and learned well – despite my professors' scathing retroactive assessment of my early education.

But I cannot blame graduate school for all the new beliefs I learned to espouse. I also learned a lot during my progressive undergraduate teacher training. There, as one of the few black education students, I learned that the open classroom was the most "humanizing" of learning environments, that children should be in control of their own learning, and that all chil-dren would read when they were ready. Determined to use all that I had learned to benefit black children, I abandoned the cornfields of Ohio, and relocated to an alternative inner-city school in Philadelphia to student-teach.

Located on the border between two communities, our "open-classroom" school deliberately maintained a popula-tion of 60 percent poor black kids from "South Philly," and 40 percent well-to-do white kids from "Society Hill." The black kids went to school there because it was their only neighbor-hood school. The white kids went to school there because their parents had learned the same kinds of things I had learned about education. As a matter of fact, there was a wait-ing list of white children to get into the school. This was unique in Philadelphia – a predominantly black school with a waiting list of white children. There was no such waiting list of black children.

I apprenticed under a gifted young kindergarten teacher. She had learned the same things that I had learned, so our pairing was most opportune. When I finished my student teaching, the principal asked me to stay on in a full-time position.

The ethos of that school was fascinating. I was one of only a few black teachers, and the other black teachers were mostly older and mostly "traditional." They had not learned the kinds of things I had learned, and the young white teachers sometimes expressed in subtle ways that they thought these teachers were – how to say it – somewhat "repressive." At the very least they were "not structuring learning environments in ways that allowed the children's intellect to flourish": they focused on "skills," they made students sit down at desks, they made students practice handwriting, they corrected oral and written grammar. The subtle, unstated message was, "They just don't realize how smart these kids are."

I was an exception to the other black teachers. I socialized with the young white teachers and planned shared classroom experiences with them. I also taught as they did. Many people told me I was a good teacher: I had an open classroom; I had learning stations; I had children write books and stories to share; I provided games and used weaving to teach math and fine motor skills. I threw out all the desks and added carpeted open learning areas. I was doing what I had learned, and it worked. Well, at least it worked for some of the children.

My white students zoomed ahead. They worked hard at the learning stations. They did amazing things with books and writing. My black students played the games; they learned how to weave; and they threw the books around the learning stations. They practiced karate moves on the new carpets. Some of them even learned how to read, but none of them as quickly as my white students. I was doing the same thing for all my kids – what was the problem?

I taught in Philadelphia for six years. Each year my teach-

ing became less like my young white friends' and more like
the other black women's who taught at the school. My students practiced handwriting; I wrote on the board; I got some
tables to replace some of the thrown-out desks. Each year my
teaching moved farther away from what I had learned, even
though in many ways I still identified myself as an open-
classroom teacher. As my classroom became more "traditional,"
however, it seemed that my black students steadily improved
in their reading and writing. But they still lagged behind. It
hurt that I was moving away from what I had learned. It hurt
even more that although my colleagues called me a good
teacher, I still felt that I had failed in the task that was most
important to me – teaching black children and teaching them
well. I could not talk about my failure then. It is difficult even
now. At least I did not fall into the trap of talking about the
parents' failures. I just did not talk about any of it.

In 1977 I left Philadelphia and managed to forget about
my quandary for six and a half years – the one and a half years
that I spent working in an administrative job in Louisiana and
the five years I spent in graduate school. It was easy to forget
failure there. My professors told me that everything I had
done in Philadelphia was right; that I was right to shun
basals; that I was right to think in terms of learner-driven and
holistic education; that, indeed, I had been a success in
Philadelphia. Of course, it was easy to forget, too, because I
could develop new focal points. I could even maintain my
political and moral integrity while doing so – graduate school
introduced me to all *sorts* of oppressed peoples who needed
assistance in the educational realm. There were bilingual
speakers of any number of languages; there were new immi-
grants. And if one were truly creative, there were even whole
countries in need of assistance – welcome to the Third World!
I could tackle someone else's failures and forget my own.

In graduate school I learned about many more elements of
progressive education. It was great. I learned new "holistic"
teaching techniques – integrating reading and writing, focusing on meaning rather than form. One of the most popular
elements – and one, I should add, which I readily and heartily

embraced – was the writing process approach to literacy. I spent a lot of time with writing process people. I learned the lingo. I focused energy on "fluency" and not on "correctness." I learned that a focus on "skills" would stifle my students' writing. I learned about "fast-writes" and "golden lines" and group process. I went out into the world as a professor of literacy armed with the very latest, research-based and field-tested teaching methods.

All went well in my university literacy classes. My student teachers followed my lead and shunned limited "traditional" methods of teaching. They, too, embraced holistic processes and learned to approach writing with an emphasis on fluency and creative expression.

But then I returned to Philadelphia for a conference. I looked up one of my old friends, another black woman who was also a teacher. Cathy had been teaching for years in an alternative high school. Most of the students in her school, and by this time in the entire Philadelphia system, were black. Cathy and I had never taught together but had worked together on many political committees and for many radical causes. We shared a lot of history, *and* a lot of philosophies. In fact, I thought we were probably in agreement on just about everything, especially everything having to do with education. I was astounded to discover our differences.

Cathy invited me to dinner. I talked about my new home, about my research in the South Pacific, and about being a university professor. She brought me up to date on all the gossip about radicals in Philly and on the new committees working against apartheid. Eventually the conversation turned to teaching, as it often does with teachers.

Cathy began talking about the local writing project based, like those in many other areas, on the process approach to writing made popular by the Bay Area Writing Project. She adamantly insisted that it was doing a monumental disservice to black children. I was stunned. I started to defend the program, but then thought better of it, and asked her why she felt so negative about what she had seen.

She had a lot to say. She was particularly adamant about the notion that black children had to learn to be "fluent" in writing – had to feel comfortable about putting pen to paper – before they could be expected to conform to any conventional standards. "These people keep pushing this fluency thing," said Cathy. "What do they think? Our children have no fluency? If they think that, they ought to read some of the rap songs my students write all the time. They might not be writing their school assignments but they sure are writing. Our kids *are* fluent. What they need are the skills that will get them into college. I've got a kid right now – brilliant. But he can't get a score on the SAT that will even get him considered by any halfway decent college. He needs *skills,* not *fluency.* This is just another one of those racist ploys to keep our kids out. White kids learn how to write a decent sentence. Even if they don't teach them in school, their parents make sure they get what they need. But what about our kids? They don't get it at home and they spend all their time in school learning to be *fluent.* I'm sick of this liberal nonsense."

I returned to my temporary abode, but found that I had so much to think about that I could not sleep. Cathy had stirred that part of my past I had long avoided. Could her tirade be related to the reasons for my feelings of past failures? Could I have been a pawn, somehow, in some kind of perverse plot against black success? What did those black nuns from my childhood and those black teachers from the school in which I taught understand that my "education" had hidden from me? Had I abrogated my responsibility to teach all of the "skills" my black students were unlikely to get at home or in a more "unstructured" environment? These were painful thoughts.

The next day at the conference I made it my business to talk to some of the people from around the country who were involved in writing process projects. I asked the awkward question about the extent of minority teacher involvement in these endeavors. The most positive answer I received was that writing process projects initially attracted a few black or minority teachers, but they soon dropped out of the program. None came back a second year. One thoughtful woman told me she had talked to some of the black teachers about their noninvolvement. She was pained about their response and still could not understand it. They said the whole thing was racist, that the meetings were racist, and that the method itself was racist. They were not able to be specific, she added, but just felt they, and their ideas, were excluded.

I have spent the last few months trying to understand all that I learned in Philadelphia. How could people I so deeply respect hold such completely different views? I could not believe that all the people from whom I had learned could possibly have sinister intentions towards black children. On the other hand, all of those black teachers could not be completely wrong. What was going on?

When I asked another black teacher in another city what she thought of her state's writing project, she replied in a huff, "Oh, you mean the white folks' project." She went on to tell me a tale I have now heard so many times. She had gone to a meeting to learn about a "new" approach to literacy. The group leaders began talking about the need for developing fluency, for first getting anything down on paper, but as soon as this teacher asked when children were to be taught the technical skills of writing standard prose, leaders of the group began to lecture her on the danger of a skills orientation in teaching literacy. She never went back.

In puzzling over these issues, it has begun to dawn on me that many of the teachers of black children have their roots in other communities and do not often have the opportunity to hear the full range of their students' voices. I wonder how many of Philadelphia's teachers know that their black students are prolific and "fluent" writers of rap songs. I wonder how many teachers realize the verbal creativity and fluency black kids express every day on the playgrounds of America as they devise new insults, new rope-jumping chants and new cheers. Even if they did hear them, would they relate them to language fluency?

Maybe, just maybe, these writing process teachers are so adamant about developing fluency because they have not really had the opportunity to realize the fluency the kids already possess. They hear only silence, they see only immobile pencils. And maybe the black teachers are so adamant against what they understand to be the writing process approach because they hear their students' voices and see their fluency clearly. They are anxious to move to the next step, the step vital to success in America – the appropriation of the oral and written forms demanded by the mainstream. And they want it to happen quickly. They see no time to waste developing the "fluency" they believe their children already possess. Yes, they are *eager* to teach "skills."

Of course, there is nothing inherent in the writing process approach itself which mitigates against students' acquiring standard literacy skills; many supporters of the approach do indeed concern themselves with the technicalities of writing in their own classrooms. However, writing process advocates often give the impression that they view the direct teaching of skills to be restrictive to the writing process at best, and at worst, politically repressive to students already oppressed by a racist educational system. Black teachers, on the other hand, see the teaching of skills to be essential to their students' survival. It seems as if leaders of the writing process movement find it difficult to develop the vocabulary to discuss the issues in ways in which teachers with differing perspectives can hear them and participate in the dialogue. Progressive white teachers seem to say to their black students, "Let me help you find your voice. I promise not to criticize one note as you search for your own song." But the black teachers say, "I've heard your song loud and clear. Now, I want to teach you to harmonize with the rest of the world." Their insistence on skills is not a negation of their students' intellect, as is often suggested by progressive forces, but an acknowledgment of it: "You know a lot; you can learn more. Do It Now!"

I run a great risk in writing this – the risk that my purpose will be misunderstood; the risk that those who subject black and other minority children to day after day of isolated, meaningless, drilled "subskills" will think themselves vindicated. That is not the point. Were this another paper I would explain what I mean by "skills" – useful and usable knowledge which contributes to a student's ability to communicate effectively in standard, generally acceptable literary forms. And I would explain that I believe that skills are best taught through meaningful communication, best learned in meaningful contexts. I would further explain that skills are a necessary but insufficient aspect of black and minority students' education. Students need technical skills to open doors, but they need to be able to think critically and creatively to participate in meaningful and potentially liberating work inside those doors. Let there be no doubt: a "skilled" minority person who is not also capable of critical analysis becomes the trainable, low-level functionary of the dominant society, simply the grease that keeps the institutions which orchestrate his or her oppression running smoothly. On the other hand, a critical thinker who lacks the "skills" demanded by employers and institutions of higher learning can aspire to financial and social status only within the disenfranchised underworld. Yes, if minority people are to effect the change which will allow them to truly progress we must insist on "skills" *within the context of* critical and creative thinking.

But that is for another paper. The purpose of this one is to defend my fellow minority educators at the same time I seek to reestablish my own place in the progressive educational arena. Too often minority teachers' voices have been hushed: a certain paternalism creeps into the speech of some of our liberal colleagues as they explain that our children must be "given voice." As difficult as it is for our colleagues to hear our children's existing voices, it is often equally difficult for them to hear our own. The consequence is that all too often minority teachers retreat from these "progressive" settings grumbling among themselves, "There they go again." It is vitally important that non-minority educators realize that there is another voice, another reality; that many of the teachers whom they seek to reach have been able to conquer the educational system *because* they received the kind of instruction that their white progressive colleagues are denouncing.

What am I suggesting here? I certainly do not suggest that the writing process approach to literacy development is wrong or that a completely skills-oriented program is right. I

suggest, instead, that there is much to be gained from the
interaction of the two orientations and that advocates of both
approaches have something to say to each other. I further suggest that it is the responsibility of the dominant group members to attempt to hear the other side of the issue; and after
hearing, to speak in a modified voice that does not exclude the
concerns of their minority colleagues.

It is time to look closely at elements of our educational system, particularly those elements we consider progressive;
time to see whether there is minority involvement and support, and if not, to ask why; time to reassess what we are doing
in public schools and universities to include other voices,
other experiences; time to seek the diversity in our educational movements that we talk about seeking in our classrooms. I would advocate that university researchers, school
districts, and teachers try to understand the views of their
minority colleagues and constituents, and that programs,
including the country's many writing projects, target themselves for study. Perhaps ethnographies of various writing
projects, with particular attention given to minority participation and nonparticipation, would prove valuable. The key
is to understand the variety of meanings available for any
human interaction, and not to assume that the voices of the
majority speak for all.

I have come to believe that the "open-classroom movement," despite its progressive intentions, faded in large part
because it was not able to come to terms with the concerns of
poor and minority communities. I truly hope that those who
advocate other potentially important programs will do a better job.

The Silenced Dialogue:
Power and Pedagogy
in Educating
Other People's Children

A black male graduate student who is also a special education teacher in a predominantly black community is talking about his experiences in predominantly white university classes:

> There comes a moment in every class where we have to discuss "The Black Issue" and what's appropriate education for black children. I tell you, I'm tired of arguing with those white people, because they won't listen. Well, I don't know if they really don't listen or if they just don't believe you. It seems like if you can't quote Vygotsky or something, then you don't have any validity to speak about your *own* kids. Anyway, I'm not bothering with it anymore, now I'm just in it for a grade.

A black woman teacher in a multicultural urban elementary school is talking about her experiences in discussions with her predominantly white fellow teachers about how they should organize reading instruction to best serve students of color:

> When you're talking to white people they still want it to be their way. You can try to talk to them and give them examples, but they're so headstrong, they think they know what's best for *everybody,* for *everybody's* children. They won't listen; white folks are going to do what they want to do *anyway.*
>
> It's really hard. They just don't listen well. No, they listen, but they don't *hear* – you know how your mama used to say you listen to the radio, but you *hear* your mother? Well they don't *hear* me.
>
> So I just try to shut them out so I can hold my temper. You can only beat your head against a brick wall for so long before you draw

blood. If I try to stop arguing with them I can't help myself from getting angry. Then I end up walking around praying all day "Please Lord, remove the bile I feel for these people so I can sleep tonight." It's funny, but it can become a cancer, a sore.

So, I shut them out. I go back to my own little cubby, my classroom, and I try to teach the way I know will work, no matter what those folk say. And when I get black kids, I just try to undo the damage they did.

I'm not going to let any man, woman, or child drive me crazy — white folks will try to do that to you if you let them. You just have to stop talking to them, that's what I do. I just keep smiling, but I won't talk to them.

A soft-spoken Native Alaskan woman in her forties is a student in the Education Department of the University of Alaska. One day she storms into a black professor's office and very uncharacteristically slams the door. She plops down in a chair and, still fuming, says, "Please tell those people, just don't help us anymore! I give up. I won't talk to them again!"

And finally, a black woman principal who is also a doctoral student at a well-known university on the West Coast is talking about her university experiences, particularly about when a professor lectures on issues concerning educating black children:

If you try to suggest that's not quite the way it is, they get defensive, then you get defensive, then they'll start reciting research.

I try to give them my experiences, to explain. They just look and nod. The more I try to explain, they just look and nod, just keep looking and nodding. They don't really hear me.

Then, when it's time for class to be over, the professor tells me to come to his office to talk more. So I go. He asks for more examples of what I'm talking about, and he looks and nods while I give them. Then he says that that's just *my* experience. It doesn't really apply to most black people.

It becomes futile because they think they know everything about everybody. What you have to say about your life, your children, doesn't mean anything. They don't really want to hear what you have to say. They wear blinders and earplugs. They only want to go on research they've read that other white people have written.

It just doesn't make any sense to keep talking to them.

Thus was the first half of the title of this text born: "The Silenced Dialogue." One of the tragedies in this field of education is that scenarios such as these are enacted daily around the country. The saddest element is that the individuals that the black and Native Alaskan educators speak of in these statements are seldom aware that the dialogue *has* been silenced. Most likely the white educators believe that their colleagues of color did, in the end, agree with their logic. After all, they stopped disagreeing, didn't they?

I have collected these statements since completing a recently published article, a somewhat autobiographical account entitled "Skills and Other Dilemmas of a Progressive Black Educator," in which I discuss my perspective as a product of a skills-oriented approach to writing and as a teacher of process-oriented approaches.[1] I described the estrangement that I and many teachers of color feel from the progressive movement when writing process advocates dismiss us as too "skills oriented." I ended the article suggesting that it was incumbent upon writing process advocates, or indeed, advocates of any progressive movement, to enter into dialogue with teachers of color, who may not share their enthusiasm about so-called new, liberal, or progressive ideas.

In response to this article, which presented no research data and did not even cite a reference, I received numerous calls and letters from teachers, professors, and even state school personnel from around the country, both black and white. All of the white respondents, except one, have wished to talk more about the question of skills versus process approaches – to support or reject what they perceive to be my position. On the other hand, *all* of the nonwhite respondents have spoken passionately on being left out of the dialogue about how best to educate children of color.

How can such complete communication blocks exist when both parties truly believe they have the same aims? How can the bitterness and resentment expressed by the educators of color be drained so that the sores can heal? What can be done?

I believe the answer to these questions lies in ethnographic analysis, that is, in identifying and giving voice to alternative worldviews. Thus, I will attempt to address the concerns raised by white and black respondents to my article "Skills and Other Dilemmas." My charge here is not to determine the best instructional methodology; I believe that the actual practice of good teachers of all colors typically incorporates a range of pedagogical orientations. Rather, I suggest that the differing perspectives on the debate over "skills" versus "process" approaches can lead to an understanding of the alienation and miscommunication, and thereby to an understanding of the "silenced dialogue."

In thinking through these issues, I have found what I believe to be a connecting and complex theme: what I have come to call "the culture of power." There are five aspects of power I would like to propose as given for this presentation:

1. Issues of power are enacted in classrooms.
2. There are codes or rules for participating in power; that is, there is a "culture of power."
3. The rules of the culture of power are a reflection of the rules of the culture of those who have power.
4. If you are not already a participant in the culture of power, being told explicitly the rules of that culture makes acquiring power easier.
5. Those with power are frequently least aware of – or least willing to acknowledge – its existence. Those with less power are often most aware of its existence.

The first three are by now basic tenets in the literature of the sociology of education, but the last two have seldom been addressed. The following discussion will explicate these aspects of power and their relevance to the schism between liberal educational movements and that of non-white, non-middle-class teachers and communities.[2]

1. Issues of power are enacted in classrooms.

These issues include: the power of the teacher over the students; the power of the publishers of textbooks and of the developers of the curriculum to determine the view of the world presented; the power of the state in enforcing compulsory schooling; and the power of an individual or group to determine another's intelligence or "normalcy." Finally, if schooling prepares people for jobs, and the kind of job a person has determines her or his economic status and, therefore, power, then schooling is intimately related to that power.

2. There are codes or rules for participating in power; that is, there is a "culture of power."

The codes or rules I'm speaking of relate to linguistic forms, communicative strategies, and presentation of self; that is, ways of talking, ways of writing, ways of dressing, and ways of interacting.

3. The rules of the culture of power are a reflection of the rules of the culture of those who have power.

This means that success in institutions — schools, workplaces, and so on — is predicated upon acquisition of the culture of those who are in power. Children from middle-class homes tend to do better in school than those from non-middle-class homes because the culture of the school is based on the culture of the upper and middle classes — of those in power. The upper and middle classes send their children to school with all the accoutrements of the culture of power; children from other kinds of families operate within perfectly wonderful and viable cultures but not cultures that carry the codes or rules of power.

4. If you are not already a participant in the culture of power, being told explicitly the rules of that culture makes acquiring power easier.

In my work within and between diverse cultures, I have come to conclude that members of any culture transmit information implicitly to co-members. However, when implicit codes are attempted across cultures, communication frequently breaks down. Each cultural group is left saying, "Why don't those people say what they mean?" as well as, "What's wrong with them, why don't they understand?"

Anyone who has had to enter new cultures, especially to accomplish a specific task, will know of what I speak. When I lived in several Papua New Guinea villages for extended periods to collect data, and when I go to Alaskan villages for work with Native Alaskan communities, I have found it unquestionably easier, psychologically and pragmatically, when some kind soul has directly informed me about such matters as appropriate dress, interactional styles, embedded meanings, and taboo words or actions. I contend that it is much the same for anyone seeking to learn the rules of the culture of power. Unless one has the leisure of a lifetime of "immersion" to learn them, explicit presentation makes learning immeasurably easier.

And now, to the fifth and last premise:

5. *Those with power are frequently least aware of — or least willing to acknowledge — its existence. Those with less power are often most aware of its existence.*

For many who consider themselves members of liberal or radical camps, acknowledging personal power and admitting participation in the culture of power is distinctly uncomfortable. On the other hand, those who are less powerful in any situation are most likely to recognize the power variable most acutely. My guess is that the white colleagues and instructors of those previously quoted did not perceive themselves to have power over the nonwhite speakers. However, either by virtue of their position, their numbers, or their access to that particular code of power of calling upon research to validate one's position, the white educators had the authority to establish what was to be considered "truth" regardless of the opinions of the people of color, and the latter were well aware of that fact.

A related phenomenon is that liberals (and here I am using the term "liberal" to refer to those whose beliefs include striving for a society based upon maximum individual freedom and autonomy) seem to act under the assumption that to make any rules or expectations explicit is to act against liberal principles, to limit the freedom and autonomy of those subjected to the explicitness.

I thank Fred Erickson for a comment that led me to look again at a tape by John Gumperz on cultural dissonance in cross-cultural interactions.[3] One of the episodes showed an

East Indian interviewing for a job with an all-white commit-tee. The interview was a complete failure, even though several of the interviewers appeared to really want to help the appli-cant. As the interview rolled steadily downhill, these "helpers" became more and more indirect in their question-ing, which exacerbated the problems the applicant had in per-forming appropriately. Operating from a different cultural perspective, he got fewer and fewer clear clues as to what was expected of him, which ultimately resulted in his failure to secure the position.

I contend that as the applicant showed less and less apti-tude for handling the interview, the power differential became ever more evident to the interviewers. The "helpful" inter-viewers, unwilling to acknowledge themselves as having power over the applicant, became more and more uncomfort-able. Their indirectness was an attempt to lessen the power differential and their discomfort by lessening the power-revealing explicitness of their questions and comments.

When acknowledging and expressing power, one tends towards explicitness (as in yelling at your ten-year-old, "Turn that radio down!"). When deemphasizing power, there is a move toward indirect communication. Therefore, in the interview setting, those who sought to help, to express their egalitarianism with the East Indian applicant, became more and more indirect – and less and less helpful – in their ques-tions and comments.

In literacy instruction, explicitness might be equated with direct instruction. Perhaps the ultimate expression of explic-itness and direct instruction in the primary classroom is Dis-tar. This reading program is based on a behaviorist model in which reading is taught through the direct instruction of phonics generalizations and blending. The teacher's role is to maintain the full attention of the group by continuous ques-tioning, eye contact, finger snaps, hand claps, and other ges-tures, and by eliciting choral responses and initiating some sort of award system.

When the program was introduced, it arrived with a flurry of research data that "proved" that all children – even those who were "culturally deprived" – could learn to read using this method. Soon there was a strong response, first from academics and later from many classroom teachers, stating that the program was terrible. What I find particularly interesting, however, is that the primary issue of the conflict over Distar has not been over its instructional efficacy – usually the students did learn to read – but the expression of explicit power in the classroom. The liberal educators opposed the methods – the direct instruction, the explicit control exhibited by the teacher. As a matter of fact, it was not unusual (even now) to hear of the program spoken of as "fascist."

I am not an advocate of Distar, but I will return to some of the issues that the program, and direct instruction in general, raises in understanding the differences between progressive white educators and educators of color.

To explore those differences, I would like to present several statements typical of those made with the best of intentions by middle-class liberal educators. To the surprise of the speakers, it is not unusual for such content to be met by vocal opposition or stony silence from people of color. My attempt here is to examine the underlying assumptions of both camps.

"I want the same thing for everyone else's children as I want for mine."

To provide schooling for everyone's children that reflects liberal, middle-class values and aspirations is to ensure the maintenance of the status quo, to ensure that power, the culture of power, remains in the hands of those who already have it. Some children come to school with more accoutrements of the culture of power already in place – "cultural capital," as some critical theorists refer to it[4] – some with less. Many liberal educators hold that the primary goal for education is for children to become autonomous, to develop fully who they are in the classroom setting without having arbitrary, outside standards forced upon them. This is a very reasonable goal for people whose children are already participants in the culture of power and who have already internalized its codes.

But parents who don't function within that culture often want something else. It's not that they disagree with the former aim, it's just that they want something more. They want to ensure that the school provides their children with discourse patterns, interactional styles, and spoken and written language codes that will allow them success in the larger society.

It was the lack of attention to this concern that created such a negative outcry in the black community when well-intentioned white liberal educators introduced "dialect readers." These were seen as a plot to prevent the schools from teaching the linguistic aspects of the culture of power, thus dooming black children to a permanent outsider caste. As one parent demanded, "My kids know how to be black – you all teach them how to be successful in the white man's world."

Several black teachers have said to me recently that as much as they'd like to believe otherwise, they cannot help but conclude that many of the "progressive" educational strategies imposed by liberals upon black and poor children could only be based on a desire to ensure that the liberals' children get sole access to the dwindling pool of American jobs. Some have added that the liberal educators believe themselves to be operating with good intentions, but that these good intentions are only conscious delusions about their unconscious true motives. One of the black anthropologist John Gwaltney's informants in *Drylongso* reflects this perspective with her tongue-in-cheek observation that the biggest difference between black folks and white folks is that black folks *know* when they're lying!

Let me try to clarify how this might work in literacy instruction. A few years ago I worked on an analysis of two popular reading programs, Distar and a progressive program that focused on higher-level critical thinking skills. In one of the first lessons of the progressive program, the children are introduced to the names of the letters *m* and *e.* In the same lesson they are then taught the sound made by each of the letters, how to write each of the letters, and that when the two are blended together they produce the word *me.*

As an experienced first-grade teacher, I am convinced that a child needs to be familiar with a significant number of these concepts to be able to assimilate so much new knowledge in one sitting. By contrast, Distar presents the same information in about forty lessons.

I would not argue for the pace of Distar lessons – such a slow pace would only bore most kids – but what happened in the other lesson is that it merely provided an opportunity for those who already knew the content to exhibit that they knew it, or at most perhaps to build one new concept onto what was already known. This meant that the child who did not come to school already primed with what was to be presented would be labeled as needing "remedial" instruction from day one; indeed, this determination would be made before he or she was ever taught. In fact, Distar was "successful" because it actually *taught* new information to children who had not already acquired it at home. Although the more progressive system was ideal for some children, for others it was a disaster.

I do not advocate a simplistic "basic skills" approach for children outside of the culture of power. It would be (and has been) tragic to operate as if these children were incapable of critical and higher-order thinking and reasoning. Rather, I suggest that schools must provide these children the content that other families from a different cultural orientation provide at home. This does not mean separating children according to family background, but instead, ensuring that each classroom incorporate strategies appropriate for all the children in its confines.

And I do not advocate that it is the school's job to attempt to change the homes of poor and nonwhite children to match the homes of those in the culture of power. That may indeed be a form of cultural genocide. I have frequently heard schools call poor parents "uncaring" when parents respond to the school's urging, saying, "But that's the school's job." What the school personnel fail to understand is that if the parents were members of the culture of power and lived by its rules and codes, then they would transmit those codes to their children. In fact, they transmit another culture that children must learn at home in order to survive in their communities.

"Child-centered, whole language, and process approaches are needed in order to allow a democratic state of free, autonomous, empowered adults, and because research has shown that children learn best through these methods."

People of color are, in general, skeptical of research as a determiner of our fates. Academic research has, after all, found us genetically inferior, culturally deprived, and verbally deficient. But beyond that general caveat, and despite my or others' personal preferences, there is little research data supporting the major tenets of process approaches over other forms of literacy instruction, and virtually no evidence that such approaches are more efficacious for children of color.[5]

Although the problem is not necessarily inherent in the method, in some instances adherents of process approaches to writing create situations in which students ultimately find themselves held accountable for knowing a set of rules about which no one has ever directly informed them. Teachers do students no service to suggest, even implicitly, that "product" is not important. In this country, students will be judged on their product regardless of the process they utilized to achieve it. And that product, based as it is on the specific codes of a particular culture, is more readily produced when the directives of how to produce it are made explicit.

If such explicitness is not provided to students, what it feels like to people who are old enough to judge is that there are secrets being kept, that time is being wasted, that the teacher is abdicating his or her duty to teach. A doctoral student of my acquaintance was assigned to a writing class to hone his writing skills. The student was placed in the section led by a white professor who utilized a process approach, consisting primarily of having the students write essays and then assemble into groups to edit each other's papers. That procedure infuriated this particular student. He had many angry encounters with the teacher about what she was doing. In his words:

> I didn't feel she was teaching us anything. She wanted us to correct each other's papers and we were there to learn from her. She didn't teach anything, absolutely nothing.

Maybe they're trying to learn what black folks knew all the time. We understand how to improvise, how to express ourselves creatively. When I'm in a classroom, I'm not looking for that, I'm looking for structure, the more formal language.

Now my buddy was in [a] black teacher's class. And that lady was very good. She went through and explained and defined each part of the structure. This [white] teacher didn't get along with that black teacher. She said that she didn't agree with her methods. But I don't think that white teacher *had* any methods.

When I told this gentleman that what the teacher was doing was called a process method of teaching writing, his response was, "Well, at least now I know that she *thought* she was doing *something*. I thought she was just a fool who couldn't teach and didn't want to try."

This sense of being cheated can be so strong that the student may be completely turned off to the educational system. Amanda Branscombe, an accomplished white teacher, recently wrote a letter discussing her work with working-class black and white students at a community college in Alabama. She had given these students my "Skills and Other Dilemmas" article to read and discuss, and wrote that her students really understood and identified with what I was saying. To quote her letter:

One young man said that he had dropped out of high school because he failed the exit exam. He noted that he had then passed the GED without a problem after three weeks of prep. He said that his high school English teacher claimed to use a process approach, but what she really did was hide behind fancy words to give herself permission to do nothing in the classroom.

The students I have spoken of seem to be saying that the teacher has denied them access to herself as the source of knowledge necessary to learn the forms they need to succeed. Again, I tentatively attribute the problem to teachers' resistance to exhibiting power in the classroom. Somehow, to exhibit one's personal power as expert source is viewed as disempowering one's students.

Two qualifiers are necessary, however. The teacher cannot be the only expert in the classroom. To deny students their own expert knowledge *is* to disempower them. Amanda Branscombe, when she was working with black high school students classified as "slow learners," had the students analyze rap songs to discover their underlying patterns. The students became the experts in explaining to the teacher the rules for creating a new rap song. The teacher then used the patterns the students identified as a base to begin an explanation of the structure of grammar, and then of Shakepeare's plays. Both student and teacher are expert at what they know best.

The second qualifier is that merely adopting direct instruction is not the answer. Actual writing for real audiences and real purposes is a vital element in helping students to understand that they have an important voice in their own learning processes. E. V. Siddle examines the results of various kinds of interventions in a primarily process-oriented writing class for black students.[6] Based on readers' blind assessments, she found that the intervention that produced the most positive changes in the students' writing was a "mini-lesson" consisting of direct instruction about some standard writing convention. But what produced the *second* highest number of positive changes was a subsequent student-centered conference with the teacher. (Peer conferencing in this group of black students who were not members of the culture of power produced the least number of changes in students' writing. However, the classroom teacher maintained — and I concur — that such activities are necessary to introduce the elements of "real audience" into the task, along with more teacher-directed strategies.)

"It's really a shame but she (that black teacher upstairs) seems to be so authoritarian, so focused on skills and so teacher directed. Those poor kids never seem to be allowed to really express their creativity. (And she even yells at them.)"

This statement directly concerns the display of power and authority in the classroom. One way to understand the difference in perspective between black teachers and their progressive colleagues on this issue is to explore culturally influenced oral interactions.

In *Ways with Words,* Shirley Brice Heath quotes the verbal

directives given by the middle-class "townspeople" teachers:[7]
  – "Is this where the scissors belong?"
  – "You want to do your best work today."
By contrast, many black teachers are more likely to say:
  – "Put those scissors on that shelf."
  – "Put your name on the papers and make sure to get the
right answer for each question."
Is one oral style more authoritarian than another?

Other researchers have identified differences in middle-
class and working-class speech to children. Snow and others,
for example, report that working-class mothers use more
directives to their children than do middle- and upper-class
parents.[8] Middle-class parents are likely to give the directive
to a child to take his bath as, "Isn't it time for your bath?"
Even though the utterance is couched as a question, both
child and adult understand it as a directive. The child may
respond with "Aw, Mom, can't I wait until...," but whether or
not negotiation is attempted, both conversants understand
the intent of the utterance.

By contrast, a black mother, in whose house I was recently a
guest, said to her eight-year-old son, "Boy, get your rusty
behind in that bathtub." Now, I happen to know that this
woman loves her son as much as any mother, but she would
never have posed the directive to her son to take a bath in the
form of a question. Were she to ask, "Would you like to take
your bath now?" she would not have been issuing a directive
but offering a true alternative. Consequently, as Heath suggests, upon entering school the child from such a family may
not understand the indirect statement of the teacher as a
direct command. Both white and black working-class children in the communities Heath studied "had difficulty inter-
preting these indirect requests for adherence to an unstated
set of rules."[9]

But those veiled commands are commands nonetheless,
representing true power, and with true consequences for dis-
obedience. If veiled commands are ignored, the child will be
labeled a behavior problem and possibly officially classified
as behavior disordered. In other words, the attempt by

the teacher to reduce an exhibition of power by expressing herself in indirect terms may remove the very explicitness that the child needs to understand the rules of the new classroom culture.

A black elementary school principal in Fairbanks, Alaska, reported to me that she has a lot of difficulty with black children who are placed in some white teachers' classrooms. The teachers often send the children to the office for disobeying teacher directives. Their parents are frequently called in for conferences. The parents' response to the teacher is usually the same. "They do what I say; if you just *tell* them what to do, they'll do it. I tell them at home that they have to listen to what you say." And so, does not the power still exist? Its veiled nature only makes it more difficult for some children to respond appropriately, but that in no way mitigates its existence.

I don't mean to imply, however, that the only time the black child disobeys the teacher is when he or she misunderstands the request for certain behavior. There are other factors that may produce such behavior. Black children expect an authority figure to act with authority. When the teacher instead acts as a "chum," the message sent is that this adult has no authority, and the children react accordingly. One reason that is so, is that black people often view issues of power and authority differently than people from mainstream middle-class backgrounds.[10] Many people of color expect authority to be earned by personal efforts and exhibited by personal characteristics. In other words, "the authoritative person gets to be a teacher because she is authoritative." Some members of middle-class cultures, by contrast, expect one to achieve authority by the acquisition of an authoritative role. That is, "the teacher is the authority because she is the teacher."

In the first instance, because authority is earned, the teacher must consistently prove the characteristics that give her authority. These characteristics may vary across cultures, but in the black community they tend to cluster around several abilities. The authoritative teacher can control the class through exhibition of personal power; establishes meaningful interpersonal relationships that garner student respect; exhibits a strong belief that all students can learn; establishes a standard of achievement and "pushes" the students to achieve that standard; and holds the attention of the students by incorporating interactional features of black communicative style in his or her teaching.

By contrast, the teacher whose authority is vested in the role has many more options of behavior at her disposal. For instance, she does not need to express any sense of personal power because her authority does not come from anything she herself does or says. Hence, the power she actually holds may be veiled in such questions/commands as "Would you like to sit down now?" If the children in her class understand authority as she does, it is mutually agreed upon that they are to obey her no matter how indirect, soft-spoken, or unassuming she may be. Her indirectness and soft-spokenness may indeed be, as I suggested earlier, an attempt to reduce the implication of overt power in order to establish a more egalitarian and nonauthoritarian classroom atmosphere.

If the children operate under another notion of authority, however, then there is trouble. The black child may perceive the middle-class teacher as weak, ineffectual, and incapable of taking on the role of being the teacher; therefore, there is no need to follow her directives. In her dissertation, Michelle Foster quotes one young black man describing such a teacher:

> She is boring, boring. She could do something creative. Instead she just stands there. She can't control the class, doesn't know how to control the class. She asked me what she was doing wrong. I told her she just stands there like she's meditating. I told her she could be meditating for all I know. She says that we're supposed to know what to do. I told her I don't know nothin' unless she tells me. She just can't control the class. I hope we don't have her next semester.[11]

But of course the teacher may not view the problem as residing in herself but in the student, and the child may once again become the behavior-disordered black boy in special education.

What characteristics do black students attribute to the good teacher? Again, Foster's dissertation provides a quotation that supports my experience with black students. A young black man is discussing a former teacher with a group of friends:

> We had fun in her class, but she was mean. I can remember she used to say, "Tell me what's in the story, Wayne." She pushed, she used to get on me and push me to know. She made us learn. We had to get in the books. There was this tall guy and he tried to take her on, but she was in charge of that class and she didn't let anyone run her. I still have this book we used in her class. It has a bunch of stories in it. I just read one on Coca-Cola again the other day.[12]

To clarify, this student was *proud* of the teacher's "meanness," an attribute he seemed to describe as the ability to run the class and pushing and expecting students to learn. Now, does the liberal perspective of the negatively authoritarian black teacher really hold up? I suggest that although all "explicit" black teachers are not also good teachers, there are different attitudes in different cultural groups about which characteristics make for a good teacher. Thus, it is impossible to create a model for the good teacher without taking issues of culture and community context into account.

And now to the final comment I present for examination:

"Children have the right to their own language, their own culture. We must fight cultural hegemony and fight the system by insisting that children be allowed to express themselves in their own language style. It is not they, the children, who must change, but the schools. To push children to do anything else is repressive and reactionary."

A statement such as this originally inspired me to write the "Skills and Other Dilemmas" article. It was first written as a letter to a colleague in response to a situation that had developed in our department. I was teaching a senior-level teacher education course. Students were asked to prepare a written autobiographical document for the class that would also be shared with their placement school prior to their student teaching.

One student, a talented young Native American woman, submitted a paper in which the ideas were lost because of technical problems – from spelling to sentence structure to paragraph structure. Removing her name, I duplicated the paper for a discussion with some faculty members. I had hoped to initiate a discussion about what we could do to ensure that our students did not reach the senior level without getting assistance in technical writing skills when they needed them.

I was amazed at the response. Some faculty implied that the student should never have been allowed into the teacher education program. Others, some of the more progressive minded, suggested that I was attempting to function as gatekeeper by raising the issue, and had internalized repressive and disempowering forces of the power elite to suggest that something was wrong with a Native American student just because she had another style of writing. With few exceptions, I found myself alone in arguing against both camps.

No, this student should not have been denied entry to the program. To deny her entry under the notion of upholding standards is to blame the victim for the crime. We cannot justifiably enlist exclusionary standards when the reason this student lacked the skills demanded was poor teaching at best and institutionalized racism at worst.

However, to bring this student into the program and pass her through without attending to obvious deficits in the codes needed for her to function effectively as a teacher is equally criminal – for though we may assuage our own consciences for not participating in victim blaming, she will surely be accused and convicted as soon as she leaves the university. As Native Alaskans were quick to tell me, and as I understood through my own experience in the black community, not only would she not be hired as a teacher, but those who did not hire her would make the (false) assumption that the university was putting out only incompetent Natives and that they should stop looking seriously at any Native applicants. A white applicant who exhibits problems is an individual with problems. A person of color who exhibits problems immediately becomes a representative of her cultural group.

No, either stance is criminal. The answer is to *accept* students but also to take responsibility to *teach* them. I decided to talk to the student and found out she had recognized that she needed some assistance in the technical aspects of writing soon after she entered the university as a freshman. She had gone to various members of the education faculty and received the same two kinds of responses I met with four years later: faculty members told her either that she should not even attempt to be a teacher, or that it didn't matter and that she shouldn't worry about such trivial issues. In her desperation, she had found a helpful professor in the English Department, but he left the university when she was in her sophomore year.

We sat down together, worked out a plan for attending to specific areas of writing competence, and set up regular meetings. I stressed to her the need to use her own learning process as insight into how best to teach her future students those "skills" that her own schooling had failed to teach her. I gave her some explicit rules to follow in some areas; for others, we devised various kinds of journals that, along with readings about the structure of the language, allowed her to find her own insights into how the language worked. All that happened two years ago, and the young woman is now successfully teaching. What the experience led me to understand is that pretending that gatekeeping points don't exist is to ensure that many students will not pass through them.

Now you may have inferred that I believe that because there is a culture of power, everyone should learn the codes to participate in it, and that is how the world should be. Actually, nothing could be further from the truth. I believe in a diversity of style, and I believe the world will be diminished if cultural diversity is ever obliterated. Further, I believe strongly, as do my liberal colleagues, that each cultural group should have the right to maintain its own language style. When I speak, therefore, of the culture of power, I don't speak of how I wish things to be but of how they are.

I further believe that to act as if power does not exist is to ensure that the power status quo remains the same. To imply to children or adults (but of course the adults won't believe you anyway) that it doesn't matter how you talk or how you write is to ensure their ultimate failure. I prefer to be honest with my students. I tell them that their language and cultural style is unique and wonderful but that there is a political power game that is also being played, and if they want to be in on that game there are certain games that they too must play.

But don't think that I let the onus of change rest entirely with the students. I am also involved in political work both inside and outside of the educational system, and that political work demands that I place myself to influence as many gatekeeping points as possible. And it is there that I agitate for change, pushing gatekeepers to open their doors to a variety of styles and codes. What I'm saying, however, is that I do not believe that political change toward diversity can be effected from the bottom up, as do some of my colleagues. They seem to believe that if we accept and encourage diversity within classrooms of children, then diversity will automatically be accepted at gatekeeping points.

I believe that will never happen. What will happen is that the students who reach the gatekeeping points – like Amanda Branscombe's student who dropped out of high school because he failed his exit exam – will understand that they have been lied to and will react accordingly. No, I am certain that if we are truly to effect societal change, we cannot do so from the bottom up, but we must push and agitate from the top down. And in the meantime, we must take the responsibility to *teach,* to provide for students who do not already possess them, the additional codes of power.[13]

But I also do not believe that we should teach students to passively adopt an alternate code. They must be encouraged to understand the value of the code they already possess as well as to understand the power realities in this country. Otherwise they will be unable to work to change these realities. And how does one do that?

Martha Demientieff, a masterful Native Alaskan teacher of Athabaskan Indian students, tells me that her students, who live in a small, isolated, rural village of less than two hundred people, are not aware that there are different codes in English. She takes their writing and analyzes it for features of what has been referred to by Alaskan linguists as "Village English," and then covers half a bulletin board with words or phrases from the students' writing, which she labels "Our Heritage Language." On the other half of the bulletin board she puts the equivalent statements in "Standard English," which she labels "Formal English."

She and the students spend a long time on the "Heritage English" section, savoring the words, discussing the nuances. She tells the students, "That's the way we say things. Doesn't it feel good? Isn't it the absolute best way of getting that idea across?" Then she turns to the other side of the board. She tells the students that there are people, not like those in the village, who judge others by the way they talk or write.

> We listen to the way people talk, not to judge them, but to tell what part of the river they come from. These other people are not like that. They think everybody needs to talk like them. Unlike us, they have a hard time hearing what people say if they don't talk exactly like them. Their way of talking and writing is called "Formal English."
>
> We have to feel a little sorry for them because they have only one way to talk. We're going to learn two ways to say things. Isn't that better? One way will be our Heritage way. The other will be Formal English. Then, when we go to get jobs, we'll be able to talk like those people who only know and can only really listen to one way. Maybe after we get the jobs we can help them to learn how it feels to have another language, like ours, that feels so good. We'll talk like them when we have to, but we'll always know our way is best.

Martha then does all sorts of activities with the notions of Formal and Heritage or informal English. She tells the students,

> In the village, everyone speaks informally most of the time unless there's a potlatch or something. You don't think about it, you don't worry about following any rules — it's sort of like how you eat food at a picnic — nobody pays attention to whether you use your fingers or a fork, and it feels *so* good. Now, Formal English is more like a formal dinner. There are rules to follow about where the knife and fork belong, about where people sit, about how you eat. That can be really nice, too, because it's nice to dress up sometimes.

The students then prepare a formal dinner in the class, for

which they dress up and set a big table with fancy tablecloths, china, silverware. They speak only Formal English at this meal. Then they prepare a picnic where only informal English is allowed.

She also contrasts the "wordy" academic way of saying things with the metaphoric style of Athabaskan. The students discuss how book language always uses more words, but in Heritage language, the shorter way of saying something is always better. Students then write papers in the academic way, discussing with Martha and with each other whether they believe they've said enough to sound like a book. Finally, students further reduce the message to a "saying" brief enough to go on the front of a T-shirt, and the sayings are put on little paper T-shirts that the students cut out and hang throughout the room. Sometimes the students reduce other authors' wordy texts to their essential meanings as well.

The following transcript provides another example. It is from a conversation between a black teacher and a Southern black high school student named Joey, who is a speaker of Black English. The teacher believes it very important to discuss openly and honestly the issues of language diversity and power. She has begun the discussion by giving the student a children's book written in Black English to read.

TEACHER: What do you think about that book?

JOEY: I think it's nice.

TEACHER: Why?

JOEY: I don't know. It just told about a black family, that's all.

TEACHER: Was it difficult to read?

JOEY: No.

TEACHER: Was the text different from what you have seen in other books?

JOEY: Yeah. The writing was.

TEACHER: How?

JOEY: It use more of a southern-like accent in this book.

TEACHER: Uhm-hmm. Do you think that's good or bad?

JOEY: Well, uh, I don't think it's good for people down this-a-way, cause that's the way they grow up talking anyway. They ought to get the right way to talk.

TEACHER: Oh. So you think it's wrong to talk like that?

JOEY: Well...{Laughs}

TEACHER: Hard question, huh?

JOEY: Uhm-hmm, that's a hard question. But I think they shouldn't make books like that.

TEACHER: Why?

JOEY: Because they are not using the right way to talk and in school they take off for that, and li'l chirren grow up talking like that and reading like that so they might think that's right, and all the time they getting bad grades in school, talking like that and writing like that.

TEACHER: Do you think they should be getting bad grades for talking like that?

JOEY: {Pauses, answers very slowly} No...no.

TEACHER: So you don't think that it matters whether you talk one way or another?

JOEY: No, not long as you understood.

TEACHER: Uhm-hmm. Well, that's a hard question for me to answer, too. It's, ah, that's a question that's come up in a lot of schools now as to whether they should correct children who speak the way we speak all the time. Cause when we're talking to each other we talk like that even though we might not talk like than when we get into other situations, and who's to say whether it's —

JOEY: {Interrupting} Right or wrong.

TEACHER: Yeah.

JOEY: Maybe they ought to come up with another kind of...maybe Black English or something. A course in Black English. Maybe Black folks would be good in that cause people talk, I mean black people talk like that, so...but I guess there's a right way and wrong way to talk, you know, not regarding what race. I don't know.

TEACHER: But who decided what's right or wrong?

JOEY: Well that's true...I guess white people did.

{Laughter. End of tape.}

Notice how throughout the conversation Joey's consciousness has been raised by thinking about codes of language. This teacher further advocates having students interview various personnel officers in actual workplaces about their attitudes toward divergent styles in oral and written language. Students begin to understand how arbitrary language standards are, but also how politically charged they are. They compare various pieces written in different styles, discuss the impact of different styles on the message by making translations and back translations across styles, and discuss the history, apparent purpose, and contextual appropriateness of each of the technical writing rules presented by their teacher. *And* they practice writing different forms to different audiences based on rules appropriate for each audience. Such a program not only "teaches" standard linguistic forms, but also explores aspects of power as exhibited through linguistic forms.

Tony Burgess, in a study of secondary writing in England by Britton, Burgess, Martin, McLeod, and Rosen, suggests that we should not teach "iron conventions...imposed without rationale or grounding in communicative intent," but "critical and ultimately cultural awareness."[14] Courtney Cazden calls for a two-pronged approach:

1. Continuous opportunities for writers to participate in some authentic bit of the unending conversation...thereby becoming part of a vital community of talkers and writers in a particular domain, and
2. Periodic, temporary focus on conventions of form, taught as cultural conventions expected in a particular community.[15]

Just so that there is no confusion about what Cazden means by a focus on conventions of form, or about what I mean by "skills," let me stress that neither of us is speaking of page after page of "skill sheets" creating compound words or identifying nouns and adverbs, but rather about helping students gain a useful knowledge of the conventions of print while engaging in real and useful communicative activities. Kay Rowe Grubis, a junior high school teacher in a multicultural school, makes lists of certain technical rules for her eighth graders' review and then gives them papers from a third grade to "correct." The students not only have to correct other students' work, but also tell them why they have changed or questioned aspects of the writing.

A village teacher, Howard Cloud, teaches his high school students the conventions of formal letter writing and the formulation of careful questions in the context of issues surrounding the amendment of the Alaska Land Claims Settlement Act. Native Alaskan leaders hold differing views on this issue, critical to the future of local sovereignty and land rights. The students compose letters to leaders who reside in different areas of the state seeking their perspectives, set up audioconference calls for interview/debate sessions, and, finally, develop a videotape to present the differing views.

To summarize, I suggest that students must be *taught* the codes needed to participate fully in the mainstream of American life, not by being forced to attend to hollow, inane, decontextualized subskills, but rather within the context of meaningful communicative endeavors; that they must be allowed the resource of the teacher's expert knowledge, while being helped to acknowledge their own "expertness" as well; and that even while students are assisted in learning the culture of power, they must also be helped to learn about the arbitrariness of those codes and about the power relationships they represent.

I am also suggesting that appropriate education for poor children and children of color can only be devised in consultation with adults who share their culture. Black parents, teachers of color, and members of poor communities must be allowed to participate fully in the discussion of what kind of instruction is in their children's best interest. Good liberal intentions are not enough. In an insightful 1975 study entitled "Racism without Racists: Institutional Racism in Urban Schools," Massey, Scott, and Dornbusch found that under the pressures of teaching, and with all intentions of "being nice," teachers had essentially stopped attempting to teach black children.[16] In their words: "We have shown that oppression can arise out of warmth, friendliness, and concern. Paternalism and a lack of challenging standards are creating a distorted system of evaluation in the schools." Educators must open themselves to, and allow themselves to be affected by, these alternative voices.

In conclusion, I am proposing a resolution for the skills/process debate. In short, the debate is fallacious; the dichotomy is false. The issue is really an illusion created initially not by teachers but by academics whose worldview demands the creation of categorical divisions – not for the purpose of better teaching, but for the goal of easier analysis. As I have been reminded by many teachers since the publication of my article, those who are most skillful at educating black and poor children do not allow themselves to be placed in "skills" or "process" boxes. They understand the need for both approaches, the need to help students establish their own voices, and to coach those voices to produce notes that will be heard clearly in the larger society.

The dilemma is not really in the debate over instructional methodology, but rather in communicating across cultures and in addressing the more fundamental issue of power, of whose voice gets to be heard in determining what is best for poor children and children of color. Will black teachers and parents continue to be silenced by the very forces that claim to "give voice" to our children? Such an outcome would be tragic, for both groups truly have something to say to one another. As a result of careful listening to alternative points of view, I have myself come to a viable synthesis of perspectives. But both sides do need to be able to listen, and I contend that it is those with the most power, those in the majority, who must take the greater responsibility for initiating the process.

To do so takes a very special kind of listening, listening that requires not only open eyes and ears, but open hearts and minds. We do not really see through our eyes or hear through our ears, but through our beliefs. To put our beliefs on hold is to cease to exist as ourselves for a moment – and that is not easy. It is painful as well, because it means turning yourself inside out, giving up your own sense of who you are, and being willing to see yourself in the unflattering light of another's angry gaze. It is not easy, but it is the only way to learn what it might feel like to be someone else and the only way to start the dialogue.

⋏ There are several guidelines. We must keep the perspective that people are experts on their own lives. There are certainly aspects of the outside world of which they may not be aware, but they can be the only authentic chroniclers of their own experience. We must not be too quick to deny their interpretations, or accuse them of "false consciousness." We must believe that people are rational beings, and therefore always act rationally. We may not understand their rationales, but that in no way militates against the existence of these rationales or reduces our responsibility to attempt to apprehend them. And finally, we must learn to be vulnerable enough to allow our world to turn upside down in order to allow the realities of others to edge themselves into our consciousness. In other words, we must become ethnographers in the true sense.

Teachers are in an ideal position to play this role, to attempt to get all of the issues on the table in order to initiate true dialogue. This can only be done, however, by seeking out those whose perspectives may differ most, by learning to give their words complete attention, by understanding one's own power, even if that power stems merely from being in the majority, by being unafraid to raise questions about discrimination and voicelessness with people of color, and to listen, no, to *hear* what they say. I suggest that the results of such interactions may be the most powerful and empowering coalescence yet seen in the educational realm – for *all* teachers and for *all* the students they teach.

Language Diversity and Learning

Abrand-new black teacher is delivering her first reading lesson to a group of first-grade students in inner-city Philadelphia. She has almost memorized the entire basal-provided lesson dialogue while practicing in front of a mirror the night before.

> "Good morning, boys and girls. Today we're going to read a story about where we live, in the city."
>
> A small brown hand rises.
>
> "Yes, Marti."
>
> Marti and this teacher are special friends, for she was a kindergartner in the classroom where her new teacher student-taught.
>
> "Teacher, how come you talkin' like a white person? You talkin' just like my momma talk when she get on the phone!"

I was that first-year teacher many years ago, and Marti was among the first to teach me the role of language diversity in the classroom. Marti let me know that children, even young children, are often aware of the different codes we all use in our everyday lives. They may not yet have learned how to produce those codes or what social purposes they serve, but children often have a remarkable ability to discern and identify different codes in different settings. It is this sensitivity to language and its appropriate use upon which we must build to ensure the success of children from diverse backgrounds.

One aspect of language diversity in the classroom — *form* (the code of a language, its phonology, grammar, inflections, sentence structure, and written symbols) — has usually received the most attention from educators, as manifested in their concern about the "nonstandardness" of the code their students speak. While form is important, particularly in the context of social success, it is considerably less important when concern is lodged instead in the area of cognitive development. This area is related to that aspect of language diversity reflected in Marti's statement – language *use* – the socially and cognitively based linguistic determinations speakers make about style, register, vocabulary, and so forth, when they attempt to interact with or achieve particular goals within their environments. It is the purpose of this paper to address a broad conception of language diversity as it affects the learning environments of linguistically diverse students; it focuses on the development of the range of linguistic alternatives that students have at their disposal for use in varying settings.

ACQUIRING ONE LANGUAGE VARIETY AND LEARNING ANOTHER

The acquisition and development of one's native language is a wondrous process, drawing upon all of the cognitive and affective capacities that make us human. By contrast, the successful acquisition of a second form of a language is essentially a rote-learning process brought to automaticity. It is, however, a process in which success is heavily influenced by highly charged affective factors. Because of the frequency with which schools focus unsuccessfully on changing language form, a careful discussion of the topic and its attendant affective aspects is in order.

The Affective Filter in Language Learning

Learning to orally produce an alternate form is not principally a function of cognitive analysis, thereby not ideally learned from protracted rule-based instruction and correction. Rather, it comes with exposure, comfort level, motivation, familiarity, and practice in real communicative contexts. Those who have enjoyed a pleasant interlude in an area where another dialect of English is spoken may have noticed a change in their own speech. Almost unconsciously, their speech has approached that of those native to the area. The evidence suggests that had these learners been corrected or drilled in the rules of the new dialect, they probably would not have acquired it as readily.

Stephen Krashen, in his work on second-language acquisition, distinguishes the processes of conscious *learning* (rule-based instruction leading to the monitoring of verbal output) from unconscious *acquisition* ("picking up" a language through internalizing the linguistic input-derived immersion in a new context — what happens, say, when the North American enjoys a visit to the Caribbean).[1] Krashen found unconscious acquisition to be much more effective. In further studies, however, he found that in some cases people did not easily "acquire" the new language. This finding led him to postulate the existence of what he called the "affective filter." The filter operates "when affective conditions are not optimal, when the student is not motivated, does not identify with the speakers of the second language, or is overanxious about his performance,...[causing] a mental block....[which]will prevent the input from reaching those parts of the brain responsible for language acquisition."[2] Although the process of learning a new dialect cannot be completely equated with learning a new language, some processes seem to be similar. In this case, it seems that the less stress attached to the process, the more easily it is accomplished.

The so-called affective filter is likely to be raised when the learner is exposed to constant correction. Such correction increases cognitive monitoring of speech, thereby making talking difficult. To illustrate with an experiment anyone can try, I have frequently taught a relatively simple new "dialect" in my work with preservice teachers. In this dialect, the phonetic element "iz" is added after the first consonant or consonant cluster in each syllable of a word. (*Teacher* becomes tiz-ea-chiz-er and *apple,* iz-ap-piz-le.) After a bit of drill and practice, the students are asked to tell a partner why they decided to become teachers. Most only haltingly attempt a few words before lapsing into either silence or into "Standard English," usually to complain about my circling the room to insist that all words they utter be in the new dialect. During a follow-up discussion, all students invariably speak of the impossibility of attempting to apply rules while trying to formulate and express a thought. Forcing speakers to monitor their language for rules while speaking, typically produces silence.

Correction may also affect students' attitudes toward their teachers. In a recent research project, middle-school, inner-city students were interviewed about their attitudes toward their teachers and school. One young woman complained bitterly, "Mrs. ———— always be interrupting to make you 'talk correct' and stuff. She be butting into your conversations when you not even talking to her! She need to mind her own business."

In another example from a Mississippi preschool, a teacher had been drilling her three- and four-year-old charges on responding to the greeting, "Good morning, how are you?" with "I'm fine, thank you." Posting herself near the door one morning, she greeted a four-year-old black boy in an interchange that went something like this:

> TEACHER: Good morning, Tony, how are you?
> TONY: I be's fine.
> TEACHER: Tony, I said, How *are* you?
> TONY: (with raised voice) I be's *fine.*
> TEACHER: No, Tony, I said *how are you?*
> TONY: (angrily) I done told you *I be's fine* and I ain't telling you no more!

Tony must have questioned his teacher's intelligence, if not sanity. In any event, neither of the students discussed above would be predisposed, as Krashen says, to identify with their teachers and thereby increase the possibility of unconsciously acquiring the latter's language form.

Ethnic Identity and Language Performance

Issues of group identity may also affect students' oral production of a different dialect. Nelson-Barber, in a study of phonologic aspects of Pima Indian language found that, in grades 1–3, the children's English most approximated the standard dialect of their teachers.[3] But surprisingly, by fourth grade, when one might assume growing competence in standard forms, their language moved significantly toward the local dialect. These fourth graders had the *competence* to express themselves in a more standard form, but chose, consciously or unconsciously, to use the language of those in their local environments. The researcher believes that, by ages 8–9, these children became aware of their group membership and its importance to their well-being, and this realization was reflected in their language. They may also have become increasingly aware of the school's negative attitude toward their community and found it necessary – through choice of linguistic form – to decide with which camp to identify.

A similar example of linguistic *performance* (what one does with language) belying linguistic *competence* (what one is capable of doing) comes from researcher Gerald Mohatt (personal communication), who was at the time teaching on a Sioux reservation. It was considered axiomatic among the reservation staff that the reason these students failed to become competent readers was that they spoke a nonstandard dialect. One day Mohatt happened to look, unnoticed, into a classroom where a group of boys had congregated. Much to his surprise and amusement, the youngsters were staging a perfect rendition of his own teaching, complete with stance, walk, gestures, *and* Standard English (including Midwestern accent). Clearly, the school's failure to teach these children to read was based on factors other than their inability to speak and understand Standard English. They could do both; they did not often choose to do so in a classroom setting, however, possibly because they chose to identify with their community rather than with the school.

APPRECIATING LINGUISTIC DIVERSITY IN THE CLASSROOM

What should teachers do about helping students acquire an additional oral form? First, they should recognize that the linguistic form a student brings to school is intimately connected with loved ones, community, and personal identity. To suggest that this form is "wrong" or, even worse, ignorant, is to suggest that something is wrong with the student and his or her family. On the other hand, it is equally important to understand that students who do not have access to the politically popular dialect form in this country, that is, Standard English, are less likely to succeed economically than their peers who do. How can both realities be embraced?

Teachers need to support the language that students bring to school, provide them input from an additional code, and give them the opportunity to use the new code in a nonthreatening, real communicative context. Some teachers accomplish this goal by having groups of students create bidialectal dictionaries of their own language form and Standard English. Others have had students become involved with standard forms through various kinds of role-play. For example, memorizing parts for drama productions will allow students to "get the feel" of speaking Standard English while not under the threat of correction. Young students can create puppet shows or role-play cartoon characters. (Many "superheroes" speak almost hypercorrect Standard English!) Playing a role eliminates the possibility of implying that the *child's* language is inadequate, and suggests, instead, that different language forms are appropriate in different contexts. Some other teachers in New York City have had their students produce a news show every day for the rest of the school. The students take on the persona of some famous newscaster, keeping in character as they develop and read their news reports. Discussions ensue about whether Walter Cronkite would have said it that way, again taking the focus off the child's speech.

ACTIVITIES FOR PROMOTING
LINGUISTIC PLURALISM

It is possible and desirable to make the actual study of language diversity a part of the curriculum for all students. For younger children, discussions about the differences in the ways television characters from different cultural groups speak can provide a starting point. A collection of the many children's books written in the dialects of various cultural groups can also provide a wonderful basis for learning about linguistic diversity, as can audiotaped stories narrated by individuals from different cultures.[4] Mrs. Pat, a teacher chronicled by Shirley Brice Heath, had her students become language "detectives," interviewing a variety of individuals and listening to the radio and television to discover the differences and similarities in the ways people talked.[5] Children can learn that there are many ways of saying the same thing, and that certain contexts suggest particular kinds of linguistic performances.

Inevitably, each speaker will make his or her own decision about the appropriate form to use in any context. Neither teachers nor anyone else will be able to force a choice upon an individual. All we can do is provide students with the exposure to an alternate form, and allow them the opportunity to practice that form *in contexts that are nonthreatening, have a real purpose, and are intrinsically enjoyable.* If they have access to alternative forms, it will be their decision later in life to choose which to use. We can only provide them with the knowledge base and hope they will make appropriate choices.

ETHNIC IDENTITY AND STYLES
OF DISCOURSE

Thus far, we have primarily discussed differences in grammar and syntax. There are other differences in oral language of which teachers should be aware in a multicultural context, particularly in discourse style and language use. Michaels and other researchers identified differences in children's narratives at "sharing time."[6] They found that there was a tendency among young white children to tell "topic-centered" narratives – stories focused on one event – and a tendency among black youngsters, especially girls, to tell "episodic" narratives – stories that include shifting scenes and are typically longer. While these differences are interesting in themselves, what is of greater significance is adults' responses to the differences. Cazden reports on a subsequent project in which a white adult was taped reading the oral narratives of black and white first graders, with all syntax dialectal markers removed.[7] Adults were asked to listen to the stories and comment about the children's likelihood of success in school. The researchers were surprised by the differential responses given by black and white adults.

In responding to the retelling of a black child's story, the white adults were uniformly negative, making such comments as "terrible story, incoherent" and "[n]ot a story at all in the sense of describing something that happened." Asked to judge this child's academic competence, all of the white adults rated her below the children who told "topic-centered" stories. Most of these adults also predicted difficulties for this child's future school career, such as, "This child might have trouble reading," that she exhibited "language problems that affect school achievement," and that "family problems" or "emotional problems" might hamper her academic progress.[8]

The black adults had very different reactions. They found this child's story "well formed, easy to understand, and interesting, with lots of detail and description." Even though all five of these adults mentioned the "shifts" and "associations" or "nonlinear" quality of the story, they did not find these features distracting. Three of the black adults selected the story as the best of the five they had heard, and all but one judged the child as exceptionally bright, highly verbal, and successful in school.[9]

When differences in narrative style produce differences in interpretation of competence, the pedagogical implications are evident. If children who produce stories based in differing discourse styles are expected to have trouble reading, and viewed as having language, family, or emotional problems, as was the case with the informants quoted by Cazden, they are unlikely to be viewed as ready for the same challenging instruction awarded students whose language patterns more closely parallel the teacher's. It is important to emphasize that those teachers in the Cazden study who were of the same cultural group as the students recognized the differences in style, but did not assign a negative valence to those differences. Thus, if teachers hope to avoid negatively stereotyping the language patterns of their students, it is important that they be encouraged to interact with, and willingly learn from, knowledgeable members of their students' cultural groups. This can perhaps best become a reality if teacher education programs include diverse parents, community members, and faculty among those who prepare future teachers, and take seriously the need to develop in those teachers the humility required for learning from the surrounding context when entering a culturally different setting.

Questioning Styles

Heath has identified another aspect of diversity in language use which affects classroom instruction and learning.[10] She found that questions were used differently in a southeastern town by young black students and their teachers. The students were unaccustomed to responding to the "known-answer" test questions of the classroom. (The classic example of such questions is the contrast between the real-life questioning routine: "What time is it?" "Two o'clock." "Thanks." and the school questioning routine: "What time is it?" "Two o'clock." *"Right!"*[11]) These students would lapse into silence or contribute very little information when teachers asked direct factual questions which called for feedback of what had just been taught. She found that when the types of questions asked of the children were more in line with the kinds of questions posed to them in their home settings – questions probing the students' own analyses and evaluations – these children responded very differently. They "talked, actively and aggressively became involved in the lesson, and offered useful information about their past experiences."[12] The author concludes not only that these kinds of questions are appropriate for all children rather than just for the "high groups" with which they have typically been used, but that awareness and use of the kinds of language used in children's communities can foster the kind of language and performance and growth sought by the school and teachers.

Oral Styles in Community Life

I would be remiss to end this section without remarking upon the need to draw upon the considerable language strengths of linguistically diverse populations. Smitherman and many others have made note of the value placed upon oral expression in most African-American communities.[13] The "man (person) of words," be he or she preacher, poet, philosopher, huckster, or rap song creator, receives the highest form of respect in the black community. The verbal adroitness, the cogent and quick wit, the brilliant use of metaphorical language, the facility in rhythm and rhyme, evident in the language of preacher Martin Luther King, Jr., boxer Muhammad Ali, comediene Whoopi Goldberg, rapper L. L. Cool J., singer and songwriter Billie Holiday, and many inner-city black students, may all be drawn upon to facilitate school learning.

Other children, as well, come to school with a wealth of specialized linguistic knowledge. Native American children, for example, come from communities with very sophisticated knowledge about storytelling, and a special way of saying a great deal with a few words. Classroom learning should be structured so that not only are these children able to acquire the verbal patterns they lack, but they are also able to strengthen their proficiencies, and to share these with classmates and teachers. We will then all be enriched.

THE DEMANDS OF SCHOOL LANGUAGE —
ORALITY AND LITERACY

There is little evidence that speaking another dialectal form per se, negatively affects one's ability to learn to read.[14] For commonsensical proof, one need only reflect on nonstandard-dialect-speaking slaves who not only taught themselves to read, but did so under threat of severe punishment or death. But children who speak nonmainstream varieties of English do have a more difficult time becoming proficient readers. Why?

One explanation is that, where teachers' assessments of competence are influenced by the dialect children speak, teachers may develop low expectations for certain students and subsequently teach them less.[15] A second explanation, which lends itself more readily to observation, rests in teachers' confusing the teaching of reading with the teaching of a new dialect form.

Cunningham found that teachers across the United States were more likely to correct reading miscues that were dialect related ("Here go a table" for "Here is a table") than those that were nondialect related ("Here is the dog" for "There is the dog").[16] Seventy-eight percent of the dialect miscues were corrected, compared with only 27 percent of the nondialect miscues. He concludes that the teachers were acting out of ignorance, not realizing that "here go" and "here is" represent the same meaning in some black children's language.

In my observations of many classrooms, however, I have come to conclude that even when teachers recognize the similarity of meaning, they are likely to correct dialect-related miscues. Consider a typical example:

TEXT: Yesterday I washed my brother's clothes.
STUDENT'S RENDITION: Yesterday I wash my bruvver close.

The subsequent exchange between student and teacher sounds something like this:

T: Wait, let's go back. What's that word again? [Points at *washed*.]

S: Wash.

T: No. Look at it again. What letters do you see at the end? You see "e-d." Do you remember what we say when we see those letters on the end of a word?

S: "ed"

T: OK, but in this case we say wash*ed*. Can you say that?

S: Wash*ed*.

T: Good. Now read it again.

S: Yesterday I wash*ed* my bruvver...

T: Wait a minute, what's that word again? [Points to *brother*.]

S: Bruvver.

T: No. Look at these letters in the middle. [Points to *th*.] Remember to read what you see. Do you remember how we say that sound? Put your tongue between your teeth and say /*th*/...

The lesson continues in such a fashion, the teacher proceeding to correct the student's dialect-influenced pronunciations and grammar while ignoring the fact that the student had to have comprehended the sentence in order to translate it into her own dialect. Such instruction occurs daily and blocks reading development in a number of ways. First, because children become better readers by having the opportunity to read, the overcorrection exhibited in this lesson means that this child will be less likely to become a fluent reader than other children who are not interrupted so consistently. Second, a complete focus on code and pronunciation blocks children's understanding that reading is essentially a meaning-making process. This child, who understands the text, is led to believe that she is doing something wrong. She is encouraged to think of reading not as something you do to get a message, but something you pronounce. Third, constant corrections by the teacher are likely to cause this student and others like her to resist reading and to resent the teacher.

Robert Berdan reports that, after observing the kind of

teaching routine described above in a number of settings, he incorporated the teacher behaviors into a reading instruction exercise that he used with students in a college class.[17] He put together sundry rules from a number of American social and regional dialects to create what he called the "language of Atlantis." Students were then called upon to read aloud in this dialect they did not know. When they made errors he interrupted them, using some of the same statements/comments he had heard elementary school teachers routinely make to their students. He concludes:

> The results were rather shocking. By the time these Ph.D. candidates in English or linguistics had read 10–20 words, I could make them sound totally illiterate. By using the routines that teachers use of dialectally different students, I could produce all of the behaviors we observe in children who do not learn to read successfully. The first thing that goes is sentence intonation: they sound like they are reading a list from the telephone book. Comment on their pronunciation a bit more, and they begin to subvocalize, rehearsing pronunciations for themselves before they dare to say them out loud. They begin to guess at pronunciations....They switch letters around for no reason. They stumble; they repeat. In short, when I attack them for their failure to conform to my demands for Atlantis English pronunciations, they sound very much like the worst of the second graders in any of the classrooms I have observed.
>
> They also begin to fidget. They wad up their papers, bite their fingernails, whisper, and some finally refuse to continue. They do all the things that children do while they are busily failing to learn to read. Emotional trauma can result as well. For instance, once while conducting this little experiment, in a matter of seconds I actually had one of my graduate students in tears.[18]

The moral of this story is not to confuse dialect intervention with reading instruction. To do so will only confuse the child, leading her away from those intuitive understandings about language that will promote reading development, and toward a school career of resistance and a lifetime of avoiding reading. For those who believe that the child has to "say it right in order to spell it right," let me add that English is not a phonetically regular language. There is no particular difference between telling a child, "You may *say* /bruvver/, but it's spelled b-r-o-*t*-*h*-e-r," and "You say /com/, but it's spelled c-o-m-*b*."

For this and other reasons, writing may be an arena in which to address standard forms. Unlike unplanned oral language or public reading, writing lends itself to editing. While conversational talk is spontaneous and must be responsive to an immediate context, writing is a mediated process which may be written and rewritten any number of times before being introduced to public scrutiny. Consequently, writing is amenable to rule application – one may first write freely to get one's thoughts down, and then edit to hone the message and apply specific spelling, syntactical, or punctuation rules. My college students who had such difficulty talking in the "iz" dialect, found writing it, with the rules displayed before them, a relatively easy task.

Styles of Literacy

There are other culturally based differences in language use in writing as well. In a seminal article arguing for the existence of "contrastive rhetoric," Robert Kaplan proposes that different languages have different rhetorical norms, representing different ways of organizing ideas.[19]

Such style differences have also been identified in public school classrooms. Gail Martin, a teacher-researcher in Wyoming, wrote about her work with Arapaho students:

> One of our major concerns was that many of the stories children wrote didn't seem to "go anywhere." The stories just ambled along with no definite start or finish, no climaxes or conclusions. I decided to ask Pius Moss [the school elder] about these stories, since he is a master Arapaho storyteller himself. I learned about a distinctive difference between Arapaho stories and stories I was accustomed to hearing, reading, and telling. Pius Moss explained that Arapaho stories are not written down, they're told in what we might call serial form, continued night after night. A "good" story is one that lasts seven nights....
>
> When I asked Pius Moss why Arapaho stories never seem to have an "ending," he answered that there is no ending to life, and stories are about Arapaho life, so there is no need for a conclusion. My col-

leagues and I talked about what Pius had said, and we decided that we would encourage our students to choose whichever type of story they wished to write: we would try to listen and read in appropriate ways.[20]

Similarly, Native Alaskan teacher Martha Demientieff has discovered that her students find "book language" baffling. To help them gain access to this unfamiliar use of language, she contrasts the "wordy," academic way of saying things with the metaphoric style of Athabaskan. The students discuss how book language always uses more words, but how in Heritage language, brevity is always best. Students then work in pairs, groups, or individually to write papers in the academic way, discussing with Martha and with each other whether they believe they have said enough to "sound like a book." Next they take those papers and try to reduce the meaning to a few sentences. Finally, students further reduce the message to a "saying" brief enough to go on the front of a T-shirt, and the sayings are put on little paper tee shirts that the students cut out and hang throughout the room. Sometimes the students reduce other authors' wordy texts to their essential meanings as well. Thus, through winding back and forth through orality and literacy, the students begin to understand the stylistic differences between their own language and that of standard text.

Functions of Print

Print may serve different functions in some communities than it does in others, and some children may be unaccustomed to using print or seeing it used in the ways that schools demand. Shirley Brice Heath, for example, found that the black children in the community she called Trackton engaged with print as a group activity for specific real-life purposes, such as reading food labels when shopping, reading fix-it books to repair or modify toys, reading the names of cars to identify a wished-for model, or reading to participate in church. There was seldom a time anyone in the community would read as a solitary recreational activity; indeed, anyone who did so was thought to be a little strange.[21]

The children in Trackton, in short, read to learn things, for real purposes. When these children arrived in school they faced another reality. They were required, instead, to "learn to read," that is, they were told to focus on the *process* of reading with little apparent real purposes in mind other than to get through a basal page or complete a worksheet – and much of this they were to accomplish in isolation. Needless to say, they were not successful at the decontextualized, individualized school reading tasks.

Researchers have identified other differences in the use of language in print as well. For example, Ron Scollon and Suzanne Scollon report that, in the Athabaskan Indian approach to communicative interaction, each individual is expected to make his or her own sense of a situation and that no one can unilaterally enforce one interpretation. Consequently, they were not surprised when, in a story-retelling exercise intended to test reading comprehension, Athabaskan children tended to modify the text of the story in their retellings.[22] The school, however, would be likely to interpret these individually constructed retellings as evidence that the students had not comprehended the story.

TALK ACROSS THE CURRICULUM

A debate over the role of language diversity in mathematics and science education was fueled recently by the publication of a book by Eleanor Wilson Orr titled *Twice as Less: Black English and the Performance of Black Students in Mathematics and Science.*[23] Orr is a teacher of math and science who, as director of the elite Hawthorne School, worked out a cooperative program with the District of Columbia to allow several Washington, D.C., public high school students to attend the prestigious school. Orr and her colleagues were dismayed to find that despite their faithfully following time-tested teaching strategies, and despite the black D.C. students' high motivation and hard work, the newcomers were failing an alarming percentage of their math and science courses.

Noting the differences in the language the black students

used, Orr decided to investigate the possibility that speaking Black English was preventing these students from excelling in math and science. In a detailed argument she contends that the students' nonstandard langauge is both the cause and the expression of the real problem — their "nonstandard *perceptions.*"[24] She cites student statements such as "So the car traveling *twice as faster* will take *twice as less* hours" to support her thesis, and suggests that it is the difference between Black English and Standard English forms in the use of prepositions, conjunctions, and relative pronouns that is the basis for the students' failures.

It is important to critique this position in order that the failures of those responsible for teaching mathematics and science to poor and black students not be attributed to the students themselves, that is, so that the victims not be blamed. There are many problems with the Orr argument. One is her assumption that black students, by virtue of speaking Black English, do not have access to certain concepts needed in mathematical problem solving. For example, she makes much of the lack of the "as ———— as" comparison, but I have recorded Black English–speaking six- to eleven-year-olds frequently making such statements as, "She big as you" and "I can too run fast as you."

A second problem is that Orr compares the language and performance of low-income, ill-prepared students with upper-income students who have had superior scholastic preparation. I contend that it was not their language which confused the D.C. students, but mathematics itself! Any students with a similar level of preparation and experience, no matter what their color or language variety, would probably have had the same difficulties.

The most basic problem with the Orr argument, however, is Orr's apparent belief that somehow mathematics is linked to the syntactical constructions of standard English: "[T]he *grammar* of standard English provides consistently for what is *true mathematically.*"[25] What about the grammar of Chinese or Arabic or German? Orr's linguistic naïve determinist position can only lead to the bizarre conclusion that speakers of other languages would be equally handicapped in mathematics because they, too, lacked standard English constructions!

Even though Orr asserts that the cause of the problem is the speaking of Black English, she seems unaware that her proposed solution is not linked to this conceptualization. She does not recommend teaching Standard English, but rather, teaching *math* through the use in instruction of irregular number systems which force students to carefully work out concepts and prevent their dependence on inappropriate rote memorized patterns. One can surmise that as students and teachers work through these irregular systems, they create a shared language, developing for the students what they truly lack, a knowledge of the *content* of the language of mathematics, not the form.

Interviews with black teachers who have enjoyed long-term success teaching math to black-dialect-speaking students suggest that part of the solution also lies in the kind and quality of talk in the mathematics classroom. One teacher explained that her black students were much more likely to learn a new operation successfully when they understood to what use the operation might be put in daily life. Rather than teach decontextualized operations, she would typically first pose a "real-life" problem and challenge the students to find a solution. For example, she once brought in a part of a broken wheel, saying that it came from a toy that she wished to fix for her grandson. To do so, she had to reconstruct the wheel from this tiny part. After the students tried unsuccessfully to solve the problem, she introduced a theorem related to constructing a circle given any two points on an arc, which the students quickly assimilated.

Another black math teacher spoke of putting a problem into terms relevant to the student's life. He found that the same problem that baffled students when posed in terms of distances between two unfamiliar places or in terms of numbers of milk cans needed by a farmer, were much more readily solved when familiar locales and the amount of money needed to buy a leather jacket were substituted. I discovered a similar phenomenon when my first-grade inner-city students did much better on "word problems" on standardized tests when I merely substituted the names of people in our school for the names in the problems.

All of these modifications to the language of instruction speak to Heath's findings in Trackton: some youngsters may become more engaged in school tasks when the language of those tasks is posed in real-life contexts than when they are viewed as merely decontextualized problem completion. Since our long-term goal is producing young people who are able to think critically and creatively in real problem-solving contexts, the instructional – and linguistic – implications should be evident.

CONCLUSION

One of the most difficult tasks we face as human beings is communicating meaning across our individual differences, a task confounded immeasurably when we attempt to communicate across social lines, racial lines, cultural lines, or lines of unequal power. Yet, all U.S. demographic data points to a society becoming increasingly diverse, and that diversity is nowhere more evident than in our schools. Currently, "minority" students represent a majority in all but two of our twenty-five largest cities, and by some estimates, the turn of the century will find up to 40 percent nonwhite children in American classrooms. At the same time, the teaching force is becoming more homogeneously white. African-American, Asian, Hispanic, and Native American teachers now comprise only 10 percent of the teaching force, and that percentage is shrinking rapidly.

What are we educators to do? We must first decide upon a perspective from which to view the situation. We can continue to view diversity as a problem, attempting to force all differences into standardized boxes. Or we can recognize that diversity of thought, language, and worldview in our classrooms cannot only provide an exciting educational setting, but can also prepare our children for the richness of living in an increasingly diverse national community. (Would any of us really want to trade the wonderful variety of American ethnic restaurants for a standard fare of steak houses and fast-food hamburgers?)

I am suggesting that we begin with a perspective that demands finding means to celebrate, not merely tolerate, diversity in our classrooms. Not only should teachers and students who share group membership delight in their own cultural and linguistic history, but all teachers must revel in the diversity of their students and that of the world outside the classroom community. How can we accomplish these lofty goals? Certainly, given the reality of the composition of the teaching force, very few educators can join Martha Demientieff in taking advantage of her shared background with her culturally unique students and contrasting "*our* Heritage language" or "the way *we* say things" with "Formal English." But teachers who do not share the language and culture of their students, or teachers whose students represent a variety of cultural backgrounds, can also celebrate diversity by making language diversity a part of the curriculum. Students can be asked to "teach" the teacher and other students aspects of their language variety. They can "translate" songs, poems, and stories into their own dialect or into "book language" and compare the differences across the cultural groups represented in the classroom.

Amanda Branscombe, a gifted white teacher who has often taught black students whom other teachers have given up on, sometimes has her middle school students listen to rap songs in order to develop a rule base for their creation. The students would teach her their newly constructed "rules for writing rap," and she would in turn use this knowledge as a base to begin a discussion of the rules Shakespeare used to construct his plays, or the rules poets used to develop their sonnets.[26]

Within our celebration of diversity, we must keep in mind that education, at its best, hones and develops the knowledge and skills each student already possesses, while at the same time adding new knowledge and skills to that base. All students deserve the right both to develop the linguistic skills they bring to the classroom and to add others to their repertoires. While linguists have long proclaimed that no language variety is intrinsically "better" than another, in a stratified society such as ours, language choices are not neutral. The language associated with the power structure – "Standard English" – is the language of economic success, and all students have the right to schooling that gives them access to that language.

While it is also true, as this chapter highlights, that no one can force another to acquire an additional language variety, there are ways to point out to students both the arbitrariness of designating one variety over another as "standard," as well as the political and economic repercussions for not gaining access to that socially designated "standard." Without appearing to preach about a future which most students find hard to envision, one teacher, for example, has high school students interview various personnel officers in actual workplaces about their attitudes toward divergent styles in oral and written language and report their findings to the entire class. Another has students read or listen to a variety of oral and written language styles and discuss the impact of those styles on the message and the likely effect on different audiences. Students then recreate the texts or talks, using different language styles appropriate for different audiences (for example, a church group, academicians, rap singers, a feminist group, politicians, and so on).

Each of us belongs to many communities. Joseph Suina, a Pueblo Indian scholar, has proposed a schematic representation of at least three levels of community membership. He sets up three concentric circles. The inner circle is labeled "home/local community," the middle circle is "national community," and the outer circle represents the "global community."[27] In today's world it is vital that we all learn to become active citizens in all three communities, and one requisite skill for doing so is an ability to acquire additional linguistic codes. We can ignore or try to obliterate language diversity in the classroom, or we can encourage in our teachers and students a "mental set for diversity." If we choose the latter, the classroom can become a laboratory for developing linguistic diversity. Those who have acquired additional codes because their local language differs significantly from the language of the national culture may actually be in a better position to gain access to the global culture than "mainstream" Americans who, as Martha says, "only know one way to talk." Rather than think of these diverse students as problems, we can view them instead as resources who can help all of us learn what it feels like to move between cultures and language varieties, and thus perhaps better learn how to become citizens of the global community.

Part 2

Lessons from Home and Abroad: Other Cultures and Communities

Lessons from Home
and Abroad:
Other Cultures and
Communities

When I consider the origins of my views, I realize that my personal history, by necessity, contributes considerably to my current belief systems. I write from a life lived in many margins, usually while struggling to approach the center of whichever page of my life is unfolding at the moment. It has been that struggle to understand and adapt to various contexts that has led me on the personal journey of discovering other realities.

My journey began early. Although I grew up in a segregated Southern community, secure as a young child that the rich tapestry of our African-American lives was not merely beautiful but the only *sensible way of functioning in the world, that tapestry unraveled quickly. When I enrolled in a newly integrated high school in the 1960s, suddenly many of the "sensible" ways of doing things no longer seemed acceptable. My fellow black classmates and I had to cope not only with the overt racism that preceded our arrival, but with the subtle racism, infinitely more insidious, that developed when aspects of our culture — language, interactional styles, belief systems — became targets for remediation at best, and evidence for our inability to learn at worst. It was then that I decided that any system that, in the name of education, did so much harm to so many children had to be changed. Those experiences also left me with a desire to understand how the world could look so different through the eyes of others.*

My attempts to reconcile my own sensibilities with the obvious differences I saw around me were only intensified as I saw more of the world. It was not until I worked in two settings most

Americans would consider exotic that I came to understand some of what was happening back at home. I spent a year conducting research in the villages of the South Pacific country of Papua New Guinea. I lived and worked with students, parents, teachers, and community members. Later, in 1984, I took my first academic job at the University of Alaska in Fairbanks, where I taught teacher education courses to white students who had moved to the far north, and to Native Alaskan students from villages and urban areas. I also spent a lot of time in remote villages visiting communities and schools. Both Papua New Guinea and Alaska forced me to approach the world very differently. I was no longer grounded in the familiar: all of my assumptions about how the world was structured didn't work.

My experiences in these geographically diverse settings were some of the most important of my life. I was very much the "other": I had no opportunity to see myself reflected in those around me. Under such circumstances, one learns to see much more clearly the assumptions one makes about the world, and to see that they are just that – assumptions. Some people in similar circumstances, I have discovered, hold on to their worldview with great tenacity, insisting that all *of the others are wrong, peculiar, undeveloped, heathen, or uncivilized. I found that my survival depended on my being willing and able to learn from my new acquaintances and my new setting, to see the world through other eyes.*

The worldviews of many in our society exist in protected cocoons. These individuals have never had to make an adjustment from home life to public life, as their public lives and the institutions they have encountered merely reflect a "reality" these individuals have been schooled in since birth. When these privileged individuals – and they are *privileged, whether they realize it or not – see others who operate from a different worldview, they can often comprehend them only as deviants, pathologically inferior, certainly in need of "fixing." Even when individuals believe themselves to have good intentions, their own biases blind them from seeing the real people before them.*

Those who have been on the receiving end of such biases under-

stand them well. I have had the opportunity to work with many teachers of color, Native Alaskan, Hispanic, and African-American. Listening to the stories of these women and men has made me even more sensitive to the ways in which most institutions in our society are created to reflect the realities of a particular cultural group — mainly the white, academically oriented middle class. Their stories have contributed, as well, to molding my views about what is needed to expand our educational vision to embrace the diversity that is this country's reality.

In this section I share some of the experiences that have shaped my beliefs. The first article, a research report of my work in Papua New Guinea, is derived from my dissertation and from reports I submitted to the Papua New Guinean government. In it, I describe the attempts of a people to make use of their own culture and language to educate their children. Their struggle has great relevance to my present work with African-American parents who push urban school systems to include African and African-American content in the curricula offered to their children. The controversy over a so-called Afrocentric curriculum may be viewed with less heat and more clarity when it is considered in an international context.

I recently wrote "Hello, Grandfather," the essay on Alaska, as I reviewed my personal journals, notes, and letters written during my four-year stay in the state. Perhaps because I am still internalizing the profound changes in worldview that my tenure there provided, this is the first piece I have written focusing specifically on Alaska. It can only begin to describe how having learned to see with other eyes has permanently changed what I am able to see.

Initially presented as a paper to the Holmes Group (an education reform group of colleges of education), the third piece in this section reports on a research project I undertook in 1987 to formally collect the views of teachers of color on their teacher education experiences and their subsequent teaching lives. My work at the time in teacher education at the University of Alaska convinced me that we need to rethink our ways of educating teachers of color if we are to have any hope of increasing their numbers in the work force. The narratives that the teachers shared and the pain they relived as they shared them cannot but help to focus attention on how education for all teachers must be reconstructed.

The Vilis Tokples Schools of Papua New Guinea

While in an Alaskan Eskimo village, I heard a young Eskimo leader speak. He had visited another area of the state where the elders of that village asked him, "Who are you?" He gave them his name, expecting that they would recognize it, as he was a gentleman of some political repute in other regions. They responded, "Yes, but who are you?" Once again he offered his name, and added his position title. They responded once more with even greater adamance, "Yes, but who are you?" Finally, he provided an account of his ancestry – his family, his tribe, his clan – placing himself in the context of all those who had come before him. The elders were finally satisfied. The young leader then explained how his education had left him ill-prepared to answer the elders' question. Had he not gone back to his own village to spend time with his grandparents after being schooled outside, he said, he would have been bewildered by the persistent questioning to the point of being unable to provide an answer.

That encounter reminded me of aspects of my own upbringing. When I return home, I am not a university professor; I am daughter, granddaughter, sister, and aunt. Unlike the academic world in which I spend most of my time, in my home world, heritage – not title and position – is central to identity. To be disconnected from that identity means losing not only the ability to explain one's essence to others but also any potential for self-knowledge as well.

We people of color must seek to find our own essence, but we must also critically examine the essence of concepts we have been taught to accept without question, such as "education" and "literacy." Can we assume that these linchpins of the "good life" are always a boon to our develop-

ment as a people? The process, context, and content of education or literacy instruction may be designed to destroy the heritage, the essence of who and what a people are, to destroy their knowledge of themselves. Education, literacy – for whom, for what purpose, toward what end? These are the questions that another people of color, Papua New Guineans of the South Pacific, asked and answered when I spent a year in their country on a travel research fellowship from Harvard University. *

Papua New Guinea, the eastern half of the second largest island in the world, is a country of astonishing contrasts, both human and geographical. The mainland and some six hundred smaller surrounding islands create a total land mass of almost three hundred thousand square miles, or over four times the total area of the six New England states. The land is so diverse that one creation myth holds that the Creator ran out of material to make an entire island, so he took a bit of every land already fashioned and formed this microcosm of the earth. The people, geographically divided into a profusion of land-locked tribal and cultural groups, live in village communities on islands, on the coast, in swampland and deltas, in upland valleys, and in the mountains. Mainly Melanesian, with some Polynesian ancestry, they vary in appearance from the curly-haired, light-complexioned, small-boned Trobriand Islanders, to the short, muscular, brown-skinned Highlanders, to the stately, sometimes blond Bougainvillians of the North Solomons Province, who may have the blackest skin of any human beings on earth.

The most widely known aspect of Papua New Guinea's diversity, however, is its multilingualism. With a little over three million people, there are over seven hundred different indigenous languages. As a former colony of Australia, the official language is English, but only about 25–30 percent of the country's population has a truly functional knowledge of the language.[1] The lingua franca spoken most widely in the

---

*I lived in the villages of a province of Papua New Guinea, from January 1981–March 1982 while I researched the effect of a mother-tongue-medium instructional program on school-community relationships, academic success, cultural change, and literacy development. I also conducted an evaluation of the program for the local government.

country, as most people's second language, is Tok Pisin. This pidgin language had its roots in "blackbirding," something closely akin to the slave trade, when Australians sometimes coerced (and often stole) Pacific Islanders away from their homes to work on Queensland plantations in the late 1800s and early 1900s.[2]

Although most widely spoken, this language has been rejected as the main language of schooling, and therefore of literacy instruction, for several reasons. Because the language has mainly been used as a trade language, in many areas it has a limited grammatical structure and vocabulary.[3] Yet even where the language has become more developed, it maintains a connection to the country's colonial past: *masta* is the Tok Pisin term for white man, *pikinini* for child, *manki* for young man, and *boi* for indigenous workman.

With the exclusion of Tok Pisin as an option, the educational language choice in Papua New Guinea, as in many other Third World countries, has been subjected to two conflicting forces: on the one hand, serving the needs of a developing nation-state with a modern exchange economy, and, on the other, serving the welfare, development, and cohesion of local, predominantly rural village communities. The needs of the former suggest English as the language of instruction and literacy, whereas the needs of the latter suggest a local language.

Another strong influence on schooling in Papua New Guinea is the region's history of literacy. Before schooling was instituted in these colonies, missionaries were surprised to discover a widespread interest in literacy. The source of that interest has been keenly debated among anthropologists. Papua New Guineans typically associated ample harvest, good fishing, and general good fortune with the ceremonial rites and rituals used to honor the spirits of ancestors. According to some accounts, in their early days of contact with Europeans some assumed that the relative riches the missionaries brought with them came from similar sources. Consequently, when workers were sent with bills of lading to the dock to pick up the missionaries' supplies from ships, they assumed that it was the writing on the paper, acting as a sort of charm, that caused the missionaries' ancestors to send such good "cargo." Later, "cargo cults" – as anthropologists called them – developed in some areas; briefly put, sect members regarded the learning of reading (usually the Bible) and writing, among other Western practices, as necessary to acquire from Papua New Guinean ancestors the goods enjoyed by the missionaries.[4]

There are stories of newly literate Papua New Guineans poring over their newly acquired Bibles in search of the secrets to obtaining the "cargo." These new literates, so the tales go, often left beaches strewn with crumpled Bible pages as they angrily accused the missionaries of having removed the important parts before handing over the texts so as to keep all the cargo for themselves.

Other researchers claim that Papua New Guinean interest in reading and writing stemmed not from a belief in charms but from a rational understanding of a new currency connected to very desirable material goods. Whatever its source, local interest in acquiring literacy was so high that some competing missions in the 1940s took to attracting new converts by staging competitive spelling bees of the previously converted. The mission whose converts won the spelling bee won the allegiance of the previously pagan onlookers. Clearly, the goal of the converts was not so much to find religious salvation as to attach themselves to the organization most likely to provide them with a skill they valued: literacy.

Schooling was first introduced by the missionaries in local languages, partially as a result of local interest and partially as a means for more efficient proselytizing. The missionaries' educational aims were not to impart secular knowledge; they wanted to teach literacy skills "so that converts could read the Bible in their village setting or be trained for the role of the pastor-teacher and catechists to spread the gospel in new places."[7]

The colonial government, on the other hand, was more concerned with the survival of the colony and the plantation economy that supported it. Achieving this goal required an indigenous population with whom plantation managers could successfully communicate and who were schooled sufficiently in the ways of the West to agree to the government's taxation and development schemes. Thus, when the government took over the role of providing education for the colony, the language of instruction changed, in most instances, to English.[6] Subsequently, literacy was taught almost exclusively in English from the 1950s on. Although at the time of independence in 1975 there was an increased interest in using local languages in schooling, the education system was run largely by Australian expatriates who questioned the practicality, and often the worth, of instruction in the medium of the mother-tongue. Consequently, English remained as the only nationally sponsored language of instruction in the nation's public schools.[7]

By the late 1970s, several concerns about schooling and school language policies had arisen — notably the cry from government officials that literacy and mathematics standards were dropping.[8] This was alternately attributed to a massive increase in the number of students served or to the recent indigenization of the teaching force. Instead of Australian and American teachers, local Papua New Guinean teachers were forced to instruct in English, a language they barely spoke and their students understood not at all. Furthermore, most of the country's children were being educated in village settings where they were unlikely ever to hear English spoken outside of the school classroom.[9]

As an increase in research on village-level thinking surfaced, a second concern about schooling arose from the residents of the villages. What researchers began to note was that even where parents actively welcomed a transforming English- and Western-focused role for the school, seeing it as a means to bring direct social and economic benefits to the community, they were unable to anticipate the disruption to social relations between young and old in rural communities that it could entail. Traditional customs, beliefs, values, and practices were devalued, leading to a sense of powerlessness, vis-à-vis the school.[10] Such feelings were poignantly expressed in the title of one study by an indigenous writer, "Education Has Robbed Me of My Child,"[11] and in a quote of an old Huli man in the Southern Highlands:

> When the Whitemen came we thought they were our ancestors returning, so how could we question their ways? They put our children inside buildings so how could we teach our forefathers' knowledge to our children when they were shut up inside and we had to stand on the outside?[12]

Even educated Papua New Guineans were feeling the tension between the pull to English associated with the modern economy, and the attachment to their own local language, reflecting their local cultural roots and values.

Yet even with this outpouring of concern about an educational language policy that was perceived as destroying the very cultural fabric of local communities, the national education system was at a loss to address the concern. With seven hundred local languages, only two hundred or so with written orthographies, how could mother-tongue education be provided for the nation's children? Once again, at the national level the educational language policy remained unchanged.

What did change was the policy of one of the country's decentralized provinces. As a result of a 1980 study conducted in the North Solomons Province, the new and innovative Vilis Tokples Pri-Skul* scheme was established in the Buka and Buin regions of the North Solomons. The program had three goals: to teach children to read, write, and count in their native language before transferring to English literacy; to give children the foundations of an education in the customs, culture, and acceptable behaviors of their community; and to teach children the basic preschool skills needed for success, in a Western sense, in the English-medium primary school.[13] The planners hoped that the bilingual, bicultural process of education would prepare children who valued and could function in both the traditional world and the newer technological world.[14]

When I arrived in the North Solomons in 1981, there were

---

*The literal translation from Tok Pisin to English would be "village talk-of-the-place pre-school."

thirty Vilis Tokples Pri-Skul schools serving approximately one thousand children in the Buka and Buin regions. Instruction was provided in the largest of the twenty-four language groups of the province. There were plans for phasing in all of the remaining languages by 1994.

❧

Separated from one another by only a shallow, half-mile strait, the tropical islands of Bougainville and Buka form a single, lush landmass that, along with a number of outlying atolls, comprise the North Solomons Province. Six hundred miles from the nation's capital, the main island is about 150 miles long and about thirty-nine miles across at its widest point. About half the land area is very hilly or mountainous, with rivers winding throughout.

The people of Bougainville-Buka can be identified by their extremely black skin, which distinguishes them from the lighter-skinned mainland Papua New Guineans whom the former refer to as "redskins." At the time of my research in the area, the population of the province numbered about 130,000, with about 82 percent of the population residing outside of the major urban areas of Arawa/Kieta and Panguna in rural, traditional villages.

The province was one of the richest in the country as a result of revenues from the large Bougainville Copper Mine at Panguna. The mine brought both wealth and independence to the province, along with a considerable amount of social unrest and the difficulties inherent in the institution of a large-scale Australian-operated enterprise in a traditional rural setting.

Educationally speaking, the North Solomons was one of the most advanced areas of the country. The province placed second on the list of provinces ranked by enrollment ratio, promotion rate, participation rate of girls, and enrollment growth.[15] Still, about two thirds of the province's children completed formal schooling at grade six when qualifying examinations were given to determine promotion. The province also had the distinction of being the first to make substantial use of educational decision-making powers it acquired through decentralization.

The indigenous people of the province were culturally and linguistically diverse. There were twenty-one different languages in the province, further divided into some forty-six sublanguages and dialects. A few old men remembered some German or Japanese expressions from the early German colonial period or from the Japanese occupation during the war, and a few of the younger men returned from other areas of the country with some knowledge of other indigenous languages, but English and Tok Pisin were the only languages not indigenous to the province that were in daily use. Most residents gained whatever knowledge they had of English from schooling, although outside of the urban areas this language was rarely spoken. Tok Pisin was known and spoken generally throughout the province, except by older people, women, and young children, who were less likely to speak it.[16]

There was some amount of distrust between inhabitants of different areas of the province, but this had been overshadowed by an even greater dislike of outsiders – the Australian "expats," and most vehemently, the "redskins," most of whom had arrived in connection with the workings of the copper mine and copra plantations.

Buka and Buin, the two regions of the North Solomons Province where the Vilis Tokples Pri-Skul scheme had thus far been initiated, were similar in their rural village lifestyles. The people's mainstay was subsistence agriculture, but recently added cash crops provided money for school fees and participation in the modern sector economy. Each area had its own form of traditional leadership that coexisted with the modern system of "community governments" set into place shortly after independence. There was also a system of village courts to handle local-level disagreements according to a not fully articulated blend of modern and traditional law.

The people of the Buka and Buin regions were also similar in their attitudes toward language. They believed it important that children knew their *tok ples* (the Tok Pisin word for indigenous language) and that they learn to read and write it so as to get along well in their villages, share knowledge with other village members articulately, participate adequately in the village court system (where oral language ability is important), write letters to friends and relatives if they left the village, and write about the community's cultural traditions in *tok ples* books. One community member in Buin believed that learning to read and write in their own language would allow children to become better thinkers, to "work out things in an intelligent, clever way as wise people do." Another Buka parent, a former teacher, believed that children should learn to read and write in *tok ples* because, as things presently stood, many children completed community school without having gained literacy in English. If they learned to read and write in *tok ples,* at least they'd be literate in some language.

Most people believed English to be more important as a *written* language than as a *spoken* language for village life. Many said that for children who remained in the villages, the ability to speak English was of little value, except when English-speaking foreigners might visit. Spoken English became important only for those young people who would leave the village to study or to seek employment. The ability to *read* and *write* English, however, could be of great value in the village, for example, to get new information from books, newspapers, and magazines, and especially to engage in business activities such as learning how to set up a trade store, order goods, and keep inventory.

Attitudes toward Tok Pisin were mixed. Frequently it was discussed as an almost necessary evil among village dwellers, and many saw it as valuable for communicating with country-men from other language areas. As such, it was a unifying force for the nation. It was also useful as a means of getting news from other areas through Radio North Solomons. Still, village people often saw Tok Pisin as less precise than either *tok ples* or English, and hence a less useful language than either. "It's not a real language. You just can't say what you want to in Tok Pisin," was a frequent complaint. The Tok Pisin used in rural areas was indeed less developed; its vocabulary was more limited than that used in urban centers so the complaint was probably justified.

People in general did not want Tok Pisin to be taught in the schools. "They learn it anyway, so why bother?" was the comment most frequently made. Some added that if children learned to read and write in *tok ples,* they would automatically gain literacy skills in Tok Pisin. (This was born out by the testing I did in Buin and Buka.[17]) The most damning attitude toward Tok Pisin, however, was the widely held belief that the prevalence of Tok Pisin was destroying the local *tok ples.* The board of management of a Buin school made the strongest statement: "Pidgin is not our language. The children learned Pidgin and they forgot our traditions."

There was a strong sense of community in the villages of Buin and Buka. Except for stricter sex-segregated activities, many of the organized social events would hardly seem out of place in a tightly knit suburban community in the United States. There were men's soccer and rugby teams and women's basketball and volleyball teams which competed with teams from neighboring villages every Sunday. Every Thursday in one village was Community Day, when all able-bodied people were to report to a central location where they were assigned tasks determined by elected committee leaders: building a cupboard for one of the teachers, cutting the grass around the school, making a new roof for a family whose house was damaged by a storm. Many people were active in the Catholic Church, both in attending services and participating in parish social activities.

Yet despite the activities introduced by missionaries which were so familiar to Western eyes, there were dramatic underlying differences. Beneath their surface appearance, the villages were deeply steeped in their own traditions. Garden crops were encouraged to produce abundantly with age-old charms; tuna-fishing boats were carried in a strictly specified manner and blessed with elaborate and secret ceremonies and sacrifices before setting out to sea. Extensive rituals for deaths, births, marriages, the building of men's custom houses, and other major events were conducted with great care and proper attention to tradition; and traditional leaders maintained an important role in village affairs.

These rites of the past coexisted with the rites of the modern era as the community went about its everyday living. Yet in other areas of existence there appeared to be a synthesis of old and new. In the area of health, for example, people seemed to trust the combined effects of the local Western-style clinic, with its injections and tablets, and the highly respected skills of the traditional healer who worked through secret charms, rituals, and local plants. In sport, as well, some young men utilized traditional "magic" in addition to daily practice sessions to ensure victory in a rugby game.

It was within this culturally integrated context that North Solomons people made it perfectly clear to a group of researchers from the University of Papua New Guinea in 1979 that what they wanted for their children was an education that prepared them to live within two cultural worlds – one that would be appropriate for those children who would stay in the village, for those who would go away and soon return, and for those who would spend most of their lives in towns and cities. They wanted "what was good from the old" so as to have children feel the security of a strong cultural base, and the "best of the new" so as to allow them to enter the changing world of towns and technology. Most of all, though, they seemed to want the privilege of making those all-important selections themselves.

Thus began the Vilis Tokples Pri-Skul scheme. In the *tokples* school, children began with two years of preschool education at age seven. They entered first grade in English-medium primary school at nine years of age and completed the six-year primary program around age fifteen.

In the *tokples* school, children learned to read, write, and count in their mother tongue and, at the same time, received a basic cultural education in the customs, values, and acceptable behavior of their community. They were prepared, as well, in the Western sense of preschooling for their primary education. Their teachers were not regularly trained teachers but instead were chosen by the local villages as best representing the values of that community and given short-course training in literacy education.

When I conducted my evaluation in 1981–82, stories about the academic and linguistic achievements of Vilis Tokples Pri-Skul children abounded. The parents and other residents of the village communities were delighted with both the program and the children's academic development. They were said to have learned a "pure" form of their local language. Several community members laughingly related how children sometimes corrected their parents' speech, which had been influenced by Tok Pisin. The children were also thought to be advanced in the skills necessary for primary school. One mother was delighted that her daughter, who had not yet entered first grade, looked closely at the family radio one night and successfully sounded out "Pa-na-so-nic." Some parents also claimed that children were better behaved, more willing to help in chores around the house, and more knowledgeable about and interested in traditional ceremonies than were their older children who did not attend Vilis Tokples Pri-Skul.

Interviews with English-medium Grade One teachers revealed that the Vilis Tokples Pri-Skul children were learning English more quickly than children in past years who had not attended Vilis Tokples Pri-Skul. The testing I conducted during my research supported the theory that children learn to read only once, and if they learn to read in a language they already understand orally, they become literate much more quickly and effectively than do those who learn in a foreign language.

Even more important to parents, however, were the social benefits of the program. Parents felt that this program allowed their children "to get along in the village." They might go on to learn English literacy and other outside knowledge, but by first learning their own language and their own cultural values, they would always "know how to live at home." One parent expressed this notion in a speech to the Parents and Citizens Board of his village:

> When children go to school, they go to an alien place, they leave their parents, they leave their gardens, they leave their homes; they leave everything that is their way of life. They sit in a classroom and

they learn things that have nothing to do with their own place. Later, because they have only learned other things, they reject their own. They don't want to dig *kau kau* [sweet potatoes], they say it's dirty; they don't want to help their mothers fetch water. They look down on these things. There are big changes in children now. They don't obey their parents, they become *rascals* [juvenile delinquents]. And this is because they have gone to school and left the things that are ours.

Now my child, he is in *tok ples* school. He is not leaving his place. He is learning in school about his customs, about his way of life. Now, he can write anything he wants to in *tok ples*. Not just things he can see, but things he thinks about, too. And he writes about his place. He writes about helping his mother carry water, about digging *kau kau*, about going to the garden. When he writes these things they become important to him. He is not only reading and writing about things outside, but learning through reading and writing to be proud of our way of life. When he is big, he will not reject us. It is important to teach our children to read and write, but it is more important to teach them to be proud of themselves, and of us.

— PARENT
LAITARO VILLAGE
Tok Ples SCHOOL
BUIN, PAPUA NEW GUINEA

These and other such statements expressed a strong feeling on the part of many parents and community members that academic education was fine and to be desired, but what really concerned them was social and moral education — the education that trains youngsters to become good people, who care about, participate in, and are proud of their communities. They saw Vilis Tokples Pri-Skuls as a means to provide that kind of education.

When I finished my research, the Vilis Tokples Skul scheme was unquestionably alive and well. It was achieving most of its immediate aims and showed promise of meeting long-range goals. The program planners and the people affected by the scheme were, by and large, happy with the results. Further, it proved that a Third World people, a black people, need not give up their culture and language to succeed in the Western world. Linguist Joshua Fishman put it well:

"The quest is for modernity...*and* authenticity, simultaneously, for seeing the *world,* but 'through our own eyes,' for going to the *world,* but 'in our own way.'"[18] It further proves that, given the opportunity, a people has every desire and capacity to participate in the planning of its future. There is never a guarantee that a particular language or educational policy will "work," but when that policy reflects the goals of the people it is to affect rather than those of either foreign missionaries or a colonial government, and when it reaffirms rather than negates a people's knowledge of its culture and heritage, then there is no better prospect for its success.

"Hello, Grandfather": Lessons from Alaska

Much scholarly research and writing focuses on disconnection. Traditional bastions of academe distance people from one another as they create power relationships whereby one group maintains the power to "name" the other. They decontextualize people as their research subjects are scrutinized and analyzed outside of their own lives. As one American Indian friend says, "I wonder how many people, as they tell stories around their campfires, know that their lives are sitting far away on someone's shelf gathering dust."

Connections and context. I learned a lot about research and I learned a lot about myself while I was in Alaska. One of the monumental lessons I learned was to reconsider my role on the earth, to understand that I could not be a distanced observer and controller of the world as academic research would have me believe. Rather, I was but one component of the world, connected to and no more important than all other parts. Once, when I was going to Denali National Park to sightsee (Denali is the Indian name for Mt. McKinley), an older Aleut friend said, "When you see the mountain, say 'Hello, Grandfather.'" That statement stopped me in my tracks: I had been going, as the superior human, to look at the lifeless, inanimate mountain. She reminded me in that brief lesson – and it was a lesson – that the mountain and I were part of the same world, that it had lived infinitely longer than I, that it would "see" me, even as I thought I was looking at it, and that I must then approach this grandfather with due respect, a respect deserved for all that it had seen.

This lesson was only one of many I received on learning to be a part of the world rather than trying to dominate it – on learning to see rather than merely to look, to feel rather than touch, to hear rather than listen: to learn, in short, about the world by being still and opening myself to experiencing it. If I realize that I am an organic part of all that is, and learn to adopt a receptive, connected stance, then I need not take an active, dominant role to understand; the universe will, in essence, include me in understanding. This realization has proved invaluable as I, an educational researcher, pursue learning about the world.

These lessons were not entirely new to me, for I come from a culture steeped in connectedness. Learning them, however, did push me to make explicit to myself aspects of my home culture, which previously had been an unexamined backdrop for everyday living.

My years of growing up fostered connectedness, as well as an understanding that things are never as they seem at any one "level of analysis." I learned early that Miss Pat, of Romper Room – no matter how much I looked into her magic mirror and no matter how good a "Do-Bee" I was – would not let me join her television classroom. "That's only for white kids," my mother explained. Things weren't as they seemed on television. She had to explain the connectedness of things initially beyond the grasp of my four-year-old, home-centered mind: somehow my "nappy" hair and my family's brown skin (I had yet to understand that my own "lighter" skin was irrelevant as long as it was embedded within a brown family) was connected to the workings of the larger world in ways that prevented me from sitting in Miss Pat's circle or from going to the bathroom while shopping downtown – and prevented my mother from trying on hats in a department store or from getting a teaching job closer to our house.

I also learned early on that my fate was irrevocably connected to that of other black people: if ever, heaven forbid, an actual or imagined crime was committed by a black person against a white person, then the well-being of all black people was at risk, often serious physical risk. We children in our segregated schools were constantly admonished about being proper "representatives of the race." The white population saw us as one undifferentiated mass, and so, perhaps, we learned to see each other that way as well. On the positive side, we therefore learned to feel like one family whether we knew each other or not, to take responsibility for caring for one another, and to take great pride in the accomplishments of our race. The sociologists and the anthropologists call it "fictive kinship"; we just called it living right. Alaska taught me to understand what I had lived.

Another lesson I learned in Alaska was the importance of context. In education, we set about solving educational problems as if they exist in a vacuum. We isolate the problem and then seek technical solutions. I was a professor of literacy in Alaska, so I was well aware of the traditional solutions for the "literacy problem" among people of color and people in the Third World. Children and adults in Alaskan villages were spoken of in much the same way as children in inner-city communities: illiteracy was high among adults, children weren't reading on their grade level (indeed, they weren't reading much at all outside of school), there was a "literacy crisis" that had to be addressed. The call for technical solutions abounded – "change the instructional methodologies": more phonics; less phonics; flood households with books, magazines, and newspapers; teach adults to read; teach parents to read to their children; encourage children to read to their parents; and so on, and so on, and so on.

Certainly some of those solutions might promote reading and writing, but I knew from my own experience that the "problem" might be deeper, related to more than the technical skills of literacy. Understanding the nature and importance of context was helpful to me not only in terms of shedding new light on the "problem"; it also helped me to understand some of the underpinnings of the Western worldview.

In our Western academic worldview, we assume that literacy is unequivocally good, and that everyone should aspire to be literate. Most of us have not taken the time to think about possible drawbacks or political implications of this ideology. Literacy can be a tool of liberation, but, equally, it can be a means of control: if the presses are controlled by the adversaries of a community, then reading can serve as a tool of indoctrination. Governments may want more people literate so that they can be held accountable for upholding laws – whether or not those laws are in the best interest of a particular community.

The practice of literacy, typically a solitary endeavor in academically oriented Western societies, can also promote alienation in communities that value collaboration and interaction. Growing up, I remember being admonished to "put that book down and go outside and play with your friends." Alaskan villages similarly value interaction and community more than individualism and solitary pursuits.

Sometimes, when I visited village classrooms I saw such conflict enacted before me. The then-accepted "best practice" in reading instruction was to abandon what many of us grew up with, "round-robin reading" – having each child read aloud in turn from a text. The savvy Anglo teachers frequently adopted these newest methods and had children read silently instead. The Native Alaskan* teachers usually adopted strategies their progressive administrators thought were outdated: they continued to have children read texts aloud as a group. Since my role as literacy instructor was to update teaching techniques, several school principals suggested that I try to get the Native teachers to change their instructional practices.

Having learned, however, the necessity of learning from the people I was supposed to teach, I presented my "suggestions" by initiating a discussion. The comments of the Native teachers were enlightening. They let me know that in order to engage their Native students and to ensure understanding of what was often a text about foreign concepts, they found it vital to read as a group. They believed that students could eventually be led to reading on their own, but that first they

---

*"Native Alaskan" and "Alaskan Native" are terms self-selected by the indigenous peoples of Alaska to represent themselves as a political group in land claims negotiations with the federal government.

needed to introduce them to the new skill and the new concepts in contexts they already found familiar, namely, interactions with people rather than with books. Connectedness was an issue once again.

Their insights reminded me, too, of work of sociolinguists and educational anthropologists such as Shirley Brice Heath, who observed a distinction between many African-American communities and middle-class white communities.* In the latter, a baby's crying resulted in someone bringing a toy for the baby to play with. In the African-American communities studied, where households tended to be more people-rich than toy-rich, someone would inevitably pick the baby up. Thus, the African-American babies early on expected people to solve their problems, while the white middle-class babies grew to connect appeasement, at least in some contexts, with objects.

When I found myself wondering how to pursue investigating whether that preference might persist as babies grew up, I asked a teacher of a multicultural group of middle-school children in Fairbanks to have her students answer a brief survey on how they would most like to learn something new. They were to rank learning from a teacher they liked, learning from a book, learning from a friend, learning from a teacher they didn't like, and learning from a computer. Sure enough, in that classroom, a higher percentage of white children preferred learning from computers and books while the African-American and Native Alaskan kids preferred human teachers. Although the sample was too small and the procedures too unscientific to come to any real conclusions, I did find the results intriguing, especially now, in light of recent recommendations to improve education in inner-city schools by shifting completely to computer-based instruction. We risk failure in our educational reforms by ignoring the significance of human connectedness in many communities of color.

---

*In no way should these examples suggest that all white people or all black people are the same. There is a great variance within any group. For example, African-American families whose lifestyles are more similar to middle-class white families have adopted more of the latter's child-rearing practices.

Spending time in Native Alaskan villages and talking with Native Alaskan teachers brought me face to face with the question of just what it takes to be successful in Western-oriented schools. How do academically oriented families train their young to be successful? How do schools reinforce and sustain what academically oriented families teach their children at home? Through readings about literacy and through my Alaskan experiences, I came to what were for me some breakthrough insights. To explain, though, I must take a rather circuitous path.

Many scholars who have studied literacy (including David Olsen, Walter Ong, Ron and Suzanne Scollon, Jack Goody and Dan Watt) have contrasted literacy with orality. Literacy communicates a message solely through a text, through the *word*. Orality, by contrast, has available to it other vehicles for communication: not only is the message transmitted through words (the text), but by factors such as the relationship of the individuals talking, where the interaction is taking place, what prior knowledge and/or understanding the participants bring to the communication encounter, the gestures used, the speaker's ability to adjust the message if the audience doesn't understand, intonation, facial expressions, and so forth – the *con,* (meaning "with,") in *context.*

Think about the difference between learning to play chess from your grandfather or learning from a book. The best part about learning from a grandfather is that there is presumably a relationship to build the learning on and, because he is there with you, he can adjust the instruction according to what he sees that you need. The problem with depending on a grandfather is that you might not have one when you need one. A book, on the other hand, transcends the necessity of the "teacher" sharing your time and space: you are in control of when you learn, even from a teacher who might be long dead. Given the hectic lives we lead in most industrialized societies, books are much easier to schedule than grandfathers.

As we pursue the increased demands and the often scheduled isolation of the modern world, there are more and more forces pulling away from sharing time and space with those we might want to learn from or communicate with. The "modern consciousness," as the Scollons would say, and its move toward greater and greater dependence upon literate communication, inevitably moves us toward a focus on "text" rather than on "context," on words rather than on all the phenomena surrounding the words.

David Olsen suggests that when children are taught to read in school, they learn both to read and to treat language as "text." Over the years, they learn, in other words, to rely less and less on contextual data and more on the decontextualized word. Jenny Cook-Gumperz says that teachers have even developed an oral style to guide children to becoming literate. By teaching children to pay attention to exact wording more than to contextualization cues in following instructions, they work toward developing skills in decontextualization that are perceived as necessary to literacy. (Even such seemingly pointless rituals as taking points off for putting one's name in the upper-left corner of the paper instead of the upper-right corner has a purpose when viewed in this light.) In schools, then – some would say in the "modern world" – the decontextualized word reigns supreme.

Not so in communities like Alaskan villages, which are more "connected" than our modern communities, and less dependent on literate means of communication. Grandfathers are usually nearby, so learning from them is more practical than learning from books. Schedules, far from isolating individuals, bring community members into frequent contact. People who work together never have to resort to memos to communicate. And news spreads from household to household without the need of newspapers.

In such communities, the *context* of a message is at least as important as, and often more important than the text of the message. It's not just what is said, but who says it, who is present when it is said, the intonation of the speaker's voice, how he or she looks when it is said, what else is happening at the same time, what happened yesterday or last week or last year.

These two contrasting communicative styles became quite evident in my own life when I moved from a predominantly white university to an historically black institution. At the white university, people tended only to listen to what you *said:* you could feel quite confident that no one would be the wiser if you expressed an entirely different message through facial expression, body language, or intonation. At the historically black university, however, I had to relearn quickly how to behave exactly as I had in my home community. People *watched* what was said as much as they listened to what was said. As a child, I could get punished for saying "yes, ma'am" while subtly "rolling" my eyes. At this institution, any gesture, any change in intonation, any slight facial expression could communicate to an audience an entirely different message than my words would suggest. Like Native Alaskans, African-Americans placed the value of context far above that of decontextualized "text."

Looking at what happened with Native teachers and children in classrooms, where the expected and approved instruction often ran counter to community expectation, helped me better understand some points of classroom cultural conflict. Jerry Mohatt, a psychologist who has worked and conducted research in many Native American communities, has captured on videotape an interesting set of interactions contrasting an Anglo teacher in a classroom of Native children, and a Native American teacher in a similar setting. What's interesting to me is the frequency with which the Anglo teacher's words do not match his actions: he frequently directs the children to do something while he is physically engaged in a completely different task himself. For example, he says, "copy the words from the board" while he is away from the blackboard looking through his desk for something or other. The Native teacher, by contrast, almost always matched her words with her actions: if she says, "copy the words," she is at the blackboard pointing. The Anglo teacher asks that the children attend to what he *says,* not what he does; the Native American teacher, on the other hand, supports her words in a related physical context. What gets *done* is at least as important as what gets said.

It would be easy to suggest that the Anglo teacher should be more consistent, but in truth he may well be unconsciously preparing children for their future schooling where they will be expected to attend to the words and not the surrounding context. Yet, if they learn what he teaches, they could find themselves in conflict with what they learn at home.

A Native Alaskan teacher commented to me that one of the most senseless rituals of schooling was the roll call: "We ask the children if they are here while looking at them!" But, of course, that conforms to the decontextualizing rituals of school: we insist that children assert their existence through the *word,* their actual presence is insufficient.

This teacher, however, developed a different kind of ritual:

> What I do is to greet all the children in the morning and talk to them. I ask them how they slept and what they had for breakfast. I also ask them what they saw on the way to school. "Did you see any clouds? Was the ground wet? Ooh, was it really cold out?" Every day I ask them about what they saw and pretty soon they begin to notice more and more because they know I'm going to ask. Then I can lead them to make connections – to learn that when a certain kind of feel is in the air then it will snow, or that when a certain kind of cloud is in the sky then the weather will change. They'll learn to learn from everything around them; they'll learn how to live in their place. And since I'm talking to them anyway, I'll mark them present!

Another example of the decontextualizing ritual often enacted in schools is our insistence that children verbally mediate any action. The action itself is not evidence of its existence – it must be put into words. Native teachers often told me that one of their greatest frustrations was to have one of their instructors in school insist that they explain how they solved a problem. Doing it was not sufficient; unless it was accompanied by words, it didn't count. How many times do we insist that children talk through some problem they have already solved? We think we are "checking for understanding," but could we merely be helping children to learn to ignore context? Could we be asking them to ignore knowledge they've acquired through a variety of nonverbal sources and to limit their understanding of the world to the word?

Ron and Suzanne Scollon, in their book *Narrative, Literacy, and Face in Interethnic Communication,* talk about their surprise in discovering how they had programmed their own daughter to focus on the decontextualized word.[1] As many linguists do, they had begun chronicling on audio tape their daughter's language development from her infancy. When they listened to the tapes they were more surprised by what *they* said than what *she* said. At one point, when the baby falls down and begins to cry, her dad scoops her up to comfort her with the words, "Aw-aw poor kid...What tripped you, did you see what tripped you?" Although the little one is not yet able to talk, she is already being taught implicitly that crying, or any reaction for that matter, is inappropriate unless it is accompanied by a verbal explanation. The Scollons discuss how so much of what just seems ordinary to academically oriented parents is really training children to respond to the world in very specific ways. While these modes may be reinforced in school, they are foreign to many children growing up in families not of part of an academic culture.

Along with valuing context, Native Alaskan communities value children in ways that many of us would find hard to fathom. We non-Natives tend to think of children as unformed future adults. We hear about the birth of a child and ask questions like, "What did she have?" "How much did it weigh?" and "Does it have any hair?" The Athabaskan Indians hear of a birth and ask, "Who came?" From the beginning, there is a respect for the newborn as a full person.

I often heard Anglo teachers in villages complain that parents don't care about their children. Nothing could have been further from the truth, yet these teachers could not see how care was manifested. They complained that parents didn't make their children come to school, yet parents believed so strongly in the necessity of respecting children's thinking that they would say that if the child did not want to come to school, then the school must not be a place that welcomed the child. The teachers said that parents didn't make the children do homework, but the parents believed that if the teacher could not present the work so that the child understood its value, then the work must have had no value. In the parents' view, children were not to be coerced with authority, but were to be treated with the respect that provided them with rationales, stated or unstated, to guide them to make decisions based on their own good sense.

During my first few years in Alaska, I was confused by a statement I heard over and over in many villages. When parents found I really wanted to hear what they had to say, they would tell me in a tone of quiet desperation, "They're making our children into robots." I accepted what they said and tried to be as sympathetic as I could while trying to understand exactly what they meant.

It wasn't until I came back to the university and talked to Eliza Jones, a gifted Athabaskan linguist, that I began to understand. Eliza, wise and educated, although not in the formal, schooled sense, told me a story – the Athabaskan way of teaching that I learned to cherish.

> A little boy went out with his grandfather and other men to hunt bear. After capturing a bear and placing it in a pit for skinning, the grandfather sent the boy for water to assist in the process. As the boy moved away from the group, his grandfather called after him, "Run, run, the bear is after you!" The boy tensed, started to run, then stopped and calmly continued walking. His grandfather called again, louder, "Run, run I say! This bear is going to catch and eat you!" But the boy continued to walk. When the boy returned with the water, his grandfather was very happy. He had passed the test.

The test the boy passed was to disregard the words of another, even those of a knowledgeable and trusted grandfather, if the information presented conflicted with his own perceptions. When children who have been brought up to trust their own observations enter school, they confront teachers, who, in their estimation, act as unbelievable tyrants. From the children's perspective, their teachers attempt to coerce behavior, even in such completely personal decisions as when to go to the bathroom or when to get a drink of water. The bell rings, go to lunch; the lights blink, put your work away, whether you are finished or not. Despite the rhetoric of American education, it does not teach children to be independent, but rather to be dependent on external sources for direction, for truth, for meaning. It trains children both to seek meaning solely from the text and to seek truth outside of their own good sense – concepts that are foreign and dangerous to Alaskan village communities.

I wonder, too, about the effect that this dependence on the decontextualized word has had on our general society. The word has the potential for becoming more and more disconnected from its surrounding context, more and more disconnected from actions. Sometimes it sees that we are moving closer and closer to the "doublespeak" of Orwell's *1984,* in which the Ministry of Love conducts war and the Ministry of Truth creates propaganda. During recent administrations the Department of Environmental Protection was led by toxic waste producers, and an era that was supposed to result in a "kinder and gentler nation" ended with more people homeless than I had ever seen in my lifetime.

In *Drylongso,* a collection of life stories from "ordinary black folks," one of the informants says to author John Gwaltney, "How can white folks talk so good and do so bad?" The informant goes on to tell a story about how a group of white cops accosts him and beats him silly. Afterward, one of them announces, "We have to get this man to the hospital." Not only is he injured and mad, but now he has a $109.50 hospital bill he can't afford to pay![2]

I do not wish to suggest by these stories that children from communities of color cannot or should not learn to become literate. Rather, I propose that those of us responsible for teaching them realize that they bring different kinds of understandings about the world than those whose home lives are more similar to the worldview underlying Western schooling. I have found that if I want to learn how best to teach children who may be different from me, then I must seek the advice of adults – teachers and parents – who are from the same culture as my students.

D., a Native teacher, told me a story about being a bilingual aide in an Anglo teacher's classroom. The teacher wanted to bring the children's culture into the class. She asked D. to write the directions for making an animal trap on the blackboard so the children could make traps in class during their activity period. D. told me she had a hard time writing up the directions, but struggled through it. The kids, however, were the ones who really had a hard time. They found the directions impossible to follow. Finally, in utter frustration, D. went home and got a trap. She took it apart and let the children watch as she put it back together. Everyone made his or her own trap in no time.

Learning solely through the decontextualized word, particularly learning something that was so much a part of their home culture, was simply too foreign for the children to grasp without careful instruction about how to make the transition. Another Native teacher told me that she handled making this transition by having the children practice writing directions to go to or from a certain place in the village. When the children finished, she took the class outside. Of course, the students wrote in ways that assumed a great deal of insider, contextual knowledge. This teacher had them laughing and trying harder and harder to be more explicit as she pretended that she was an outsider, a *gussak* (white person) trying to get her knowledge solely from the text. They soon understood that they had to use words in a different way in order to get their message across.

She repeated the exercise with other familiar activities over the year, such as having the children write down how to make different Native foods and then having them watch her attempt to follow the directions. After a while, the children learned that they could make use of decontextualized literacy when they needed to. They did not learn, however, that they had to give up their own contextual way of experiencing the world.

Other Native teachers made literacy learning a group rather than a solitary endeavor. There was much time spent talking and discussing what was read, particularly when the text presented concepts foreign to the children's physical setting or to their background knowledge. Many Native and sensitive Anglo teachers also devised reading and writing activities that would in some way contribute to the well-being of the community. Some had students write letters to senators about the Native Land Claims Settlement Act or to the Fish and Game Department about some new ruling that was adversely affecting the village subsistence economy. In short, the successful teachers of Native Alaskan children found ways to contextualize the literate endeavors and to celebrate, rather than to limit, the sense of connectedness which the children brought to school.

Unfortunately, most Native Alaskan children do not have Native Alaskan teachers, just as most children of color throughout this country do not have teachers from their own cultural group. A young Athabaskan Indian boy once looked at his teacher and asked, "When are we going to die?" The teacher to whom he addressed the question was surprised, but answered, "Well, none of us know when we are going to die, that is for a power beyond us to decide." The young boy looked away and said softly, "Well, if we don't know when we are going to die, then why do we have to go to school? Why can't we just be happy?" That Native Alaskan teacher later said to me with tears in her eyes, "Why can't we figure out ways to make that child happy in school?"

Touched by those comments, I have carried around the question of that child and that teacher for many years. Why do we have such a hard time making school a happy place for poor children and children of color? A few years ago, I asked Oscar Kwageley, a friend, teacher, Yupik Eskimo scientist, and wise man, what the purpose of education is. His response startled me and opened my eyes even more: he said, "The purpose of education is to learn to die satiated with life." That, I believe, is what we need to bring to our schools: experiences that are so full of the wonder of life, so full of connectedness, so embedded in the context of our communities, so brilliant in the insights that we develop and the analyses that we devise, that all of us, teachers and students alike, can learn to live lives that leave us truly satisfied.

Teachers' Voices: Rethinking Teacher Education for Diversity

There can be no doubt that issues of diversity form the crux of what may be one of the biggest challenges yet to face those of us whose business it is to educate teachers. In the wake of reports proposing the complete reformation of teacher education has come a groundswell of concern about the effects of reform-related activities on the participation of ethnically and culturally diverse teachers in the workforce.[1]

Concern is not misplaced; conservative estimates suggest that black, Hispanic, Asian, and Native American children presently comprise almost 30 percent of the school-age population, and "minority" students represent a majority in all but two of our twenty-five largest cities. Furthermore, by some estimates the turn of the century will find up to 40 percent nonwhite children in American classrooms.[2] Yet the current number of teachers from nonwhite groups threatens to fall below 10 percent, and the percentage of education degrees conferred onto members of these groups decreased by more than 6 percent between 1981 and 1985; additional data suggest a continued downward trend.[3] Patricia Graham, then dean of Harvard's Graduate School of Education, put it succinctly: "Most teachers who teach today's children are white; tomorrow's teaching force will be even more so."[4]

Researchers have cited many reasons for the decline of minority participation in the teaching force – among them, the overall decline of the numbers of college-bound students from ethnic groups, the widening of professional opportunities for people of color, the increased prevalence of competency examinations, the lack of prestige for teaching as a profession, low salaries, and less than optimal working conditions. Numerous recommendations have been made to try to remedy the situation: providing increased financial aid to students of color, recruiting nontraditional college students (for example, military retirees), providing "test-wiseness" instruction to increase the passing rates on various state or institution-mandated examinations, raising teacher salaries, and restructuring schools to provide teachers with more autonomy and more opportunities for career advancement. While many of these recommendations have proven useful, the problem still exists.

In the course of defining the problem and seeking viable solutions, we in the research community have seldom looked to teachers themselves as major sources of guidance. When ethnically diverse teachers are asked to reflect on "the problem," additional dimensions come to the fore. The following personal statements were collected in the course of conducting research about the attitude of educators of color toward their preservice and in-service teacher education, and their subsequent teaching lives:

An African-American elementary teacher on her teacher education experience in a predominantly white institution:

> My teacher education was just a joke. I did everything I was supposed to do, but they weren't impressed. I was just too confident and outspoken. So I said to myself, "I guess I have to play their game." I had to shuffle my feet; Lisa, I literally had to grin and bow! And then I got an A. This was my freshman year. I was the only black person in the class. Coming from the inner city, where at least teachers would treat you kind of fair, I thought these people could give me constructive criticism. That's all I ever asked for. I know I'm not perfect. White people — I guess it's going to sound racist — but white people want black people to be humble, to be grateful they gave them a little bit of time. Usually I just can't do it, but I should have gotten the Academy Award for my performance [in teacher education classes]! So to me, the joke started then and went on for four years.

A Native Alaskan teacher is talking about her teacher training experiences:

I must have heard this so many times, that Native kids are low achievers. It used to frustrate me to hear that, and here I used to think, *what they don't know.* What I thought was that these "educators" have never really been out there. They just went by what they learned from books.

I had a hang-up about this for a long time. I used to try to strike back without realizing what I was saying. Finally I started to say to myself, "In order to get through this thing, I have to pass this course, even though they're talking about *me.*"

This is happening in my graduate classes right now. They're talking about Native kids, and I relate it to me – "low achievers," "high dropouts," "they don't function well academically." We are labeled right from the beginning. I hear these things about my people and I get so frustrated.

An African-American woman who left teaching talks about her cooperating teacher:

She thought all black children were poor, but the kids in that school weren't poor. She kept talking about how we couldn't expect too much from them because they were poor. She even thought *I* was poor. She kept asking me questions like, "Is your father unemployed a lot?"

A Native Alaskan teacher speaking on what she learned in teacher education courses:

I only learned how to teach white kids. I didn't learn one thing about teaching Native kids. It *is* different, you know. But I don't think they even thought about that.

Clearly, in some sense, these educators feel themselves to be victimized by the institutions that seek to educate them. They believe their voices to be unheard, their concerns unheeded. The intent of the ongoing research described herein is to collect those voices and concerns in order to assist those of us in teacher education to better address the needs of preservice and in-service teachers of color. It is my hope as well that the findings will provide insights into how to better prepare those from the larger culture to teach the increasingly diverse student bodies they are likely to face in the course of their careers.

The data were collected in twelve in-depth, two-hour ethnographic interviews with six African-American and six Native American teachers or former teachers (see page 193 of the Notes section for the open-ended interview schedule), supplemented by five shorter telephone interviews with black teachers, and a group meeting with Native Alaskan teachers.[5]

What do people of color have to say about their experiences as preprofessional and professional educators? Despite the diverse ethnicities and backgrounds represented in the sample, the teachers interviewed showed surprising consensus on several points:

1. Most of the black and Native teachers interviewed believe accounts of their own experiences are not validated in teacher education programs or in their subsequent teaching lives.

A Native teacher who graduated in 1985 said that at the university there was no communication between the other non-Native students and herself or between her instructors and herself, "except to tell me that I did something wrong. I never felt I could say anything." She added that her sister, whom she described as usually assertive, quit the university because "no one would listen to her." This teacher also complained about courses outside the education department, particularly about history courses which she believed presented a one-sided view of the world:

> Those history books just said, "The Russians set up camp in Ruby" [an Alaskan village]. Nowhere did they talk about how they killed Natives for sport or stole women from their families and forced them to get married. My own Aunt ——— was one of those women. They [the professors and students] just couldn't see the other side. Finally, in all my classes I just gave up and decided to learn what they said to learn, so I could get out. If they said 2 + 2 = 5, I learned that. If they said Christopher Columbus discovered America, I regurgitated it back to them.

Another Native teacher, who completed teacher education in 1973 but never entered the teaching profession, reported that during her teacher education she always thought she should "shut up and forget about it" when people said things she knew were wrong:

But then I started saying, "How come we can't say anything?" Then, when I tried to talk, they always said I didn't make sense. I kept hearing, "Could you explain yourself more?"

Later, I began to think I must be a radical or a racist or something because *they* always said, "Everything's great, why make a fuss." I'd say, *"No, it's not!"*

Students of color are doubly disadvantaged in trying to get their voices heard, particularly in the university classroom. First, the university does not as a rule value personal narratives as having a legitimate cognitive function. Discourse in the university setting is more valued if it reflects independence of context, analysis, and objectification of experience. Such a style is more associated with written text, and consequently an oral mode that calls upon the written for validation (that is, citing previously recorded research) is more valued.

Because these students' experiences have not, in general, been so codified, they typically have no written text available upon which to call. Furthermore, they are often members of cultural groups for which narrative is the preferred means of information transfer.[6] Thus, students find themselves feeling, as one African-American said, that the university professors and students "only want to go by research they've read that other white people have written," and that "if you can't quote Vygotsky…, then you don't have any validity to speak about your *own* kids." Cazden paraphrases an Alaskan Tlingit Indian woman in graduate school at Harvard:

> When someone, even an undergraduate, raises a question that is based on what some authority says, Professor X says, "That's a great question!", expands on it, and incorporates it into her following comments. But when people like me talk from our personal experience, our ideas are not acknowledged. The professor may say, "Hm-hm," and then proceed as if we hadn't been heard.[7]

A second reason that the stories of students of color may go unheard or unvalidated is that, as some scholars suggest, true performance of narrative is connected to such factors as similar background and a shared sense of identity.[8] Therefore, narratives are most likely to be "heard" or considered legitimate when they are shared among people who consider themselves in some way comembers of a group.[9] To the extent that people of color (or students in general, for that matter) are not considered comembers of the university professor's group, it is unlikely that their personal narratives will be valued. Additional evidence suggests that, indeed, teachers of color do not feel that in the university or in their subsequent teaching lives their own cultural groups are considered to be of equal status with the dominant culture. This is further discussed with the next generalization gleaned from the interviews.

2. The teachers interviewed frequently encountered negative and/or stereotypical cultural and racial attitudes directed toward themselves and toward ethnic minority children during their teacher education and subsequent teaching lives.

Every one of the teachers interviewed related experiencing some form of what they considered to be racial bias.[10] Three interviewees who left the teaching profession entirely cite these experiences as their major reasons for leaving:

A forty-one-year-old black man who completed his math/science education degree in 1969, spoke of leaving teaching after two years in a junior high school in Alabama:

> I left teaching because I got totally dissatisfied with the system I was a part of. The staff was 98 percent white and 2 percent black. Near the end of the first year, I realized that I was the only staff member interested in helping *students* progress, not in just covering the course material. I found I had to teach reading before I could teach science. I started asking questions: "Why hadn't the faculty taught the basics?" Eventually, I started telling faculty they weren't doing their job.
>
> The black kids were bussed as a result of desegregation. They got the kids there, all right, but nobody cared about them once they got there. Finally I left because it was too much to handle. I couldn't get through to the staff that they were hurting kids. People really didn't care about black kids, whether they learned or not. There was so much inequality. Black kids just weren't given the attention they needed.
>
> The other teachers and the department head thought we [he and the other black science teacher] were rabble-rousers because we kept

pushing them to really teach black kids....In a way, I'm sorry I quit, but then I probably would have gotten fired anyway.

A Native woman who completed teacher education in 1973, decided not to enter teaching after graduation. To be sure, part of her decision was based on another job offer, but she declared that her primary reason for leaving was her experience in student teaching:

> The teachers at ———— [a boarding school for Native students] had the attitude that the students were hard to teach. Some told me that they didn't think the [Native] kids knew *how* to think. One teacher told me he'd give me a million dollars if I could figure out how to teach these kids. Now I know that there is a way, I should go back and collect! It wasn't that the kids couldn't think, it was that [those teachers] couldn't teach....
>
> From student teaching, I realized what kind of treatment I'd get from the other teachers – they wouldn't even let me use the Xerox machine. I expected that if I went into teaching, the other teachers would all tell me everything I was doing wrong. It was just too discouraging.

She added that, based on her own experience and her children's experiences in village schools, she knew that the teachers always separated themselves from the village people. "I'd have to choose sides – either with the teachers or with the village – and I'd choose the village. It would be too hard being in the middle like that."

The third nonteaching education graduate, a black woman who completed college in 1964 but decided not to begin a teaching career, also cites her student teaching experience as the reason she chose not to enter the profession:

> The school in which I did my student teaching, ———— High School in Detroit, was in transition from middle-class Jewish to black. The school was tracked. The highest track was all white, the middle track was mixed, and the lowest track was all black....There was no attempt to understand black children, to reach these children or to make positive educational experiences for them. They would just tolerate them at best.
>
> My cooperating teacher was just ruinous for black kids. She was ruinous for low-achieving black kids. She had no notion of how to

build self-esteem, or even that she should. In her opinion, the bright kids deserved attention, and she was there to prove that the others couldn't learn.

After that one semester of student teaching, I felt I just couldn't work in the public school system. The system was corrupt, and I'd be fighting and fussing the whole time. No, the system was murderous. It didn't exist to educate children. I realized it was bigger than me, and I had to leave.

Other interviewees encountered attitudes of bias that can be organized into four categories: bias toward children of color by nonminority teachers; bias against the interviewee by parents and/or children in a predominantly white school; bias toward the interviewee by other teachers; and bias toward the interviewee or stereotypic attitudes directed toward his or her cultural group by the university curriculum, professors, or fellow students. None of the interviewees reported experiencing bias in all four categories, but all cited experience in at least one.

Several comments about negative attitudes expressed toward children have been cited above. Another black teacher complained of a white teacher who loudly chastised two Athabaskan Indian children in the hallway, referring to them as "wild Indians."

Four teachers commented that white children and/or parents sometimes questioned their authority. A Native junior high school teacher reported that during her first year of teaching some white children would ask derisively, "Who hired you?" One black and two Native teachers said that white parents were more likely to seek conferences with them than with their white colleagues, were more likely to wish to observe their teaching (in some instances, even when they did not have children in the interviewee's classroom!), and were more likely to complain about their teaching.

Five teachers felt discriminated against at one time or another by their white colleagues, ranging from stereotyping (one black teacher complained that during student teaching her cooperating teacher wanted to know if her family was on welfare) to feelings of isolation (a Native teacher reported that she hung around the teachers' lounge for weeks in a large predominantly white high school without getting to know even one other teacher).

Perhaps the most poignant story is from a young Native woman who was in her first year of teaching. She was the only Native teacher at an elementary school with a black woman principal. She said that some of the other teachers resented her because they perceived the African-American principal as providing her with preferential treatment:

> It's difficult being the only Native here. I was an aide here before I received my degree, and everyone was very nice. Now I get a lot of resentment from the staff. I think it's because they resent the fact that a Native was hired [in a tight job market]; they think it should have been a white person.
>
> They don't give my degree as much credibility. Two teachers set up a meeting with me after school and told me I wasn't doing my job. They said I was the principal's favorite so she's not telling me all the things I'm doing wrong. It's people like that who intimidate me. I went home feeling bad about myself, feeling so incompetent.
>
> I even think some teachers pick on my students because they're my kids. I feel so excluded. They don't share anything with me. I found my own material, developed my own style to show them I could do it.

Finally, six teachers cited the fourth kind of biased behavior in their experiences in the university during their teacher education. Negative attitudes in the university appear to be expressed in two ways: directly toward the student, and/or more generally toward the student's cultural group. This bias can be classified, according to Benokraitis and Feagin's scheme of discrimination, as "overt" (most blatant), "covert" (clandestine, maliciously motivated), and "subtle" (unequal treatment that is visible but so internalized as to be considered routine in bureaucratized settings).[11]

Two of the teachers reported overt discrimination from their professors, who implied they were not sufficiently competent to complete the university program. One black teacher was told, for example, "You're not really capable of doing this work. You're only here because somebody paid your way." Another black teacher talked about what she perceived as covert discrimination when, during her teacher education, a group of professors met (without her knowledge) to discuss how to get her to resign from the program.

The most common experience of bias at the university falls into the category of subtle discrimination. The interviewees refer to such discrimination when they complain of the lack of credence given to their words and opinions. In addition, Native interviewees particularly complained that some of their instructors exhibited what Mehrabian has labeled "low immediacy" behaviors when interacting with them: "colder" voice tone, less eye contact, and distanced body orientation.[12] One of these educators commented that such behavior "made me feel like I wasn't there." Another said that she felt like the professor wanted her to "just disappear."

Several interviewees criticized professors, students, and the curriculum for perpetuating stereotypes about people of color. This kind of discrimination is exemplified by the comments of a Native woman who objected when a fellow student declared in class that one could not expect Native children to speak in a classroom "because they're just not like that, they're very silent." The people from her region, she counters, "are *very* vocal, and children are taught to be vocal, too." She continued:

> I resented those kinds of stereotypes about Native children. I remember in a reading class there was a discussion. The generalization was made that Native children coming from a village are a lot slower than white children living in town, and that you've got to expect this and you've got to expect that. And really, when everybody knows the clout of teacher expectations, people who say that really burn me up. They develop a very narrow view, a stereotype of how a Native child is. They don't really look at that child as a person, but as a Native. That was one thing I struggled with as well, people supposing things about me before getting to know me.

Another Native teacher said that "reading all those studies about 'the plight of Native students' made me feel like part of a group of people who were failures and I was the one exception. Why do they do that? I guess that's one way for a dominant culture to maintain dominance – not to recognize any of the strengths of another group." (It is sobering to realize that most of what concerns these teachers was probably added to the curriculum in an attempt to address issues of cultural diversity.)

Several researchers have observed that there are large numbers of nonwhite teachers who are certified to teach but are not teaching.[13] Consequently, those who seek to increase the numbers of teachers of color cannot only recruit new minority students to teacher education programs; they must identify why teachers leave the profession. If these interviews are in any way representative of the larger population, in order to recruit and *retain* teachers of color, schools of education must find means to address what these teachers perceive as racial discrimination during teacher education and beyond.

It is not easy to fulfill such a charge, in part because racial discrimination in present-day America is less likely to be the overt, blatant bigotry of the past. In a review of the survey data on racial attitudes gathered from 1942 to 1983, for example, another group of researchers has documented that there have indeed been major changes in white stereotypes of blacks and in abstract principles applied to racial issues: in 1942 only 42 percent of those whites surveyed believed that blacks had the same intelligence as whites. By 1956 that percentage increased to 80 percent, where it remained until the study was conducted.[14] Again, in 1942 only 42 percent of whites surveyed thought blacks "should have as good a chance as white people to get any kind of job"; by 1972, 97 percent did so.[15]

However, despite change in the stated beliefs of the white population, recent studies depict their actions as reflecting other values. Researchers have found that the reactions of whites to people of color display subtle discriminatory behavior: less assistance, greater aggression, overt friendliness coupled with covert rejection, avoidance, and assessment inconsistent with actual work performance.[16] Furthermore, whites are seldom conscious of this "modern prejudice," even as they practice it. Pettigrew and Martin discuss the ramifications of modern prejudice for black professionals:

> Precisely because of their subtlety and indirectness, these modern
> forms of prejudice and avoidance are hard to eradicate. Often the
> black is the only person in a position to draw the conclusion that
> prejudice is operating in the work situation. Whites have usually
> observed only a subset of the incidents, any one of which can be
> explained away by a nonracial account. Consequently, many whites
> remain unconvinced of the reality of subtle prejudice and discrimi-
> nation, and come to think of their black coworkers as "terribly
> touchy" and "overly sensitive" to the issue. For such reasons, the
> modern forms of prejudice frequently remain invisible even to its
> {sic} perpetrators.[17]

Furthermore, the issue is apparently not just one of biased
expectations and evaluations. Some researchers have demonstrated that bias can actually *cause* lowered performance for
those who are its victims, possibly as a result of unexpressed
anger, alienation, low morale, and other mental and physical
symptoms of stress.[18] It is easy to anticipate how such lowered
performance can readily lead to even greater stereotyping and
bias, thus increasing the minority person's sense of alienation
and frustration. And in an age of proliferating competency
examinations, perhaps actually lowering achievement potential as well.

*3. The teachers interviewed report significant differences from their
white colleagues in classroom pedagogy and discipline, saying that
their teaching styles are most influenced by their own experiences as
learners, their reflections about their students, and from the culture
bearers in their community.*
    In an informal survey of a class of graduate students, four-
teen of fifteen white teachers named external sources as having
the most influence on their present teaching styles: either a
role model (typically a childhood teacher or a cooperating
teacher during student teaching) or an in-service education
class (such as a writing project). This is in line with other findings which suggest that the majority of teachers tend to
model their teaching on methodological orientations taught
in teacher education or on other practicing teachers they have
encountered.[19]

This is in sharp contrast to the teachers of color interviewed. All but one of these teachers cited internal sources of knowledge as a primary basis for their own teaching: reflections on their own experiences as learners or their own ability to assess and create. When an external source was cited, it was typically a nonformally-educated culture bearer in the teacher's community. In response to questions about what influenced their teaching style most, teachers' statements reflect these perspectives:

> I tried to remember how I learned. I teach the way I learned, not the way I was taught.

> I created my teaching from my own personal concerns – what was important to improve the condition of black people.

> I knew how to teach Native children because I went through the same frustrations they went through.

> I brought to mind remnants from how I was taught – and then I did the opposite.

> My own experiences as a student influenced me the most.

> My own self-determination – my ability to monitor, adjust, make things interesting.

> I knew my culture and that's what helped me to know how to teach. I spent time with community people, particularly my mom – and she brought to mind what I had learned.

> My mother. I think about how she raised her children and try to treat my students like that. She has influenced my style the most, even though she never went to college.

The one teacher whose comments did not fit into this general pattern was a black man whose own education, from elementary school through college, was in all-black settings. He spoke of his black teachers as role models: "I learned to teach from them; sometimes you have to see a master at work. I taught science the way I was taught science."

With the exception of this one man, a primary reason for

the lack of external models for those interviewed may be the perception of a significant difference between themselves and other teachers in what constitutes good teaching. To summarize their responses, the teachers interviewed believed that what they encountered in their own careers as students, pre-service teachers, and in-service teachers, was not often good teaching in their estimation. By contrast, they declared that:

1. Good teachers care whether students learn. They challenge all students, even those who are less capable, and then help them to meet the challenge.
2. Good teachers are not time-bound to a curriculum and do not move on to new subject matter until all students grasp the current concept.
3. Good teachers are not bound to books and instructional materials, but connect all learning to "real life."
4. Good teachers push students to think, to make their own decisions.
5. Good teachers communicate with, observe, and get to know their students and the students' cultural background.

Black and Native teachers alike expressed similar beliefs. Interestingly, although the question was not framed in racial terms, when asked how their teaching differed from the other educators around them, almost all the teachers responded by contrasting their conception of good teaching with that of white teachers (probably because the teachers interviewed taught in predominantly white settings). In order to clarify the distinctions they made, the teachers often called upon their experiences as learners:

A black principal of eleven years who taught junior high science for four years: White teachers follow the curriculum in books and don't make it relevant. They apply it to the future – to what they'll need in college. But many kids don't go on to college. How can they use it now?

A black teacher of twelve years: I think everybody should be challenged. We work hard, but it's not boring. When the other teachers get a child who's a little slower they just let them sit there. I refuse to let even one child vegetate in my room.

A Native woman who decided not to teach after becoming certified: In high school I had only one Native teacher who taught American History. She made us *think.* She let us do all the talking. She used to say, "If you don't talk, who's going to talk for you; if you don't think, who's going to think for you?" I was surprised she told us we had to think. No other teacher had ever said that to us.

A Native teacher who graduated in 1985 and taught for two years: The books were alien to me, so I figured they'd be alien to the kids. I taught differently from the white teachers. I put a lot of Alaska into it. I taught the books, but I always put it in the present tense – showed the kids how what we read about was connected to me and to them....Some of the white teachers were very nice; it's just that they are so into the books, books, books.

A black woman who decided not to teach after becoming certified: I had a really second-rate education in junior high and high school. Most of my teachers were white. Their approach was to pat us on the back and tell us we were fine. Nothing was required. They just gave up on us....Once I had a black teacher who was really tough – but I loved her because she *cared.* She even dared to flunk people. She made us do difficult tasks, made us think hard about what we were doing. The others thought we didn't need schooling because we'd never be anything anyway, so there was no need to worry about teaching.

A black retired mathematics teacher: You have to justify what you want kids to learn. You have to show them how they'll use it. I got interested in math because my grandfather used to be a carpenter. He'd show me how to do all the calculations to build things. I showed my students how each thing I asked them to learn was useful to real life. White teachers want to get through the book, but I think it's more important to *really* learn a *few* things than to *not* learn a *lot* of things.

A black teacher who taught for two years and left the profession in 1971: Other staff felt that the most important thing was to get through the book. We [he and a black coworker] didn't try to cover the book. The department head said you have to cover the material – *x* number of pages in the semester. We said, why leave a chapter until it's fully covered and everyone understands the basic concepts? She wanted us to move on, thought we weren't teaching properly....I like to challenge kids. Sometimes you open up an area and kids get excited. I think you should let kids explore a topic. I'd stay on it for a week, ask them what they wanted to do with it, where they think we should go....My [black] science teacher always asked questions. You had to *think* in his class. He was always asking questions. He wouldn't just give it to you, you had to think and be creative. That's how I teach.

A Native teacher of two years: If there's someone who doesn't understand what I'm teaching, I try to understand who they are.

A black elementary principal who taught for seven years: My philosophy is, if it's boring to me, it's boring for the kids. I tried to make things fun, but realistic, rooted in the kids' real lifestyle. Then I integrated skills into all of that. Minority teachers bring in realistic things, white teachers are more superficial, more book-oriented. Minority teachers expect kids to make their own decisions; white teachers tell kids everything to do. Minority teachers say, "What do *you* think you need to do?" The kids have to make the decision.

A black teacher who now works in an administrative central office position: With my black elementary teachers you had to talk just like in a Baptist church. You have to *talk* to the preacher. There's got to be a dialogue. If you don't feel comfortable with your students, you won't do this. My instructors [in a black college] knew what you knew because they talked to you. They *knew* the students. That's really the only way to teach....Teaching is all about telling a story. You have to get to know kids so you'll know how to tell the story, you can't tell it just one way. You can tell if you're on the right track by watching the kids. If their facial expressions aren't right, change the story.

A black teacher of seven years: You have to know the kids. They teach me how to teach them. They may be from all kinds of backgrounds and cultures, but if you really listen to them, they'll tell you how to teach them.

A middle-aged Native teacher who has taught in a village for two years: They [white teachers in the school] keep waiting for some program on a white horse to ride in and save them. I focus on the kids, think about what I didn't know at their age and teach that.

A first-year Native teacher in a multicultural urban setting: I believe that the curriculum guides aren't the Bible. I'm teaching kids, not books. The teachers move through the books whether the kids get it or not, so I end up getting minority kids who can't read.... I use the curriculum guide, but move beyond it. I make the story connect to the kids' real lives.

A Native teacher who taught in a village for three years and then moved into bilingual education administration: You have to have high expectations. If you challenge kids, they'll do what you want. Tell them they can all get *A*s, then tell them how to do it. They'll work for you if you challenge them and help them get there.

In addition to these highly consistent statements about pedagogy, the Native teachers also observed that their disciplinary styles were different from those of dominant culture teachers. They told of getting into trouble with their administrators for not forcefully demanding obedience from their pupils. The teachers seem to believe that it is unnecessary and exceptionally rude to shout at students or to use other coercive means to control behavior. They preferred to allow students to have opportunities to vent frustrations or to disagree with stated rules. When it was necessary to change behavior, they sought to do so by appealing to affiliation rather than authority. "Our people don't act like that" was often the unstated message.

Given the teachers' perspective that their own ideas about teaching are so different from what they consider to be the mainstream norm, it is not surprising that most of those interviewed spoke of teacher education as just something "to get through" rather than as something to learn from. When the teachers spoke of learning anything during the experience, it was likely to be subject area knowledge or the more technical or more superficial aspects of the profession, for example, writing lesson plans, giving tests, learning the jargon, gaining an understanding of mainstream values, learning "how to act like a teacher" – and, as one teacher put it, "learning to bullshit." This lack of true involvement in the teacher education experience can only have been exacerbated by the final generalized factor to be discussed.

4. The teachers interviewed often felt isolated from instructors and other students during their teacher training.

Because of the communication difficulties between instructors and students, many of the students of color felt that they were not able to talk to many of their white professors. The Native teachers, in particular, found communication with professors and other students difficult. Four dropped out of college (although they later returned), in part because they felt so isolated in the dormitories and in classrooms:

> You get awfully lonely when no one can or will communicate with you. A lot of Native students run home and never come back. Others turn to drugs and alcohol just to fill the emptiness. Many don't make it, but those that go through have to learn to find companionship.

Six of the interviewees found professors of color to provide that companionship, and in several instances, these individuals became the interviewees' only motivation to remain in school. These professors established what the students perceived to be a human and caring relationship in a generally indifferent environment, and also served as role models for what they might become:

> I had one Native teacher in college, and this is where I relaxed and where I didn't have to feel pushed. My colleague, a Native from Kiana, and I used to just sit in there and say, "Oh what a relief to come to this class where we're not being threatened by so many things – academically, by words, all those uppity words. Here we can really talk to the teacher and we're able to talk our own language and work toward something we enjoy."

> Professor ———, at the University, was a role model for me – just to see a Native teaching. I always looked forward to going to his classes. I never went up to him to talk, but just seeing him made me want to go on. There was one black professor who was also a friend. I could talk to that professor about my frustrations. That's the only way I made it through.

One teacher had been enrolled in a special field-delivered, village-based teacher education program in which there was strong focus on using the village as a source of knowledge and in which the professors established individual tutoring relationships with the students. She reported that these white male professors were primarily responsible for her completing the program:

> Those teachers were just bothersome. It seemed like they knew when I was on the verge of quitting and they just showed up at my door. They spent so many hours with me. I started thinking that if *they* thought I could do it, then I could do it. They really cared. I really finished for them – it's like I owed it to them.

It is clear that the interviewees' difficulties are complicated by issues of cultural background, class, and individual differences, but if we wish to address the problem, we must give credibility to these educators' *perceptions* of the problem.

How can teacher education programs be expected to do that? First, given these teachers' response to the presence of faculty of color (that is, a reduced sense of isolation and alienation, an increased comfort level, and a sense of having an ally and/or role model), we would do well to seek to diversify our faculties. Members of a diverse faculty can also assist each other in understanding the needs of – and avoiding unintentional slights or insults to – diverse students; no individual can be expected to understand the intricacies of every culture without the assistance of members from those cultures.

Until schools of education can reach that apparently elusive goal of an ethnically representative faculty, however, the results from one interview suggest that nonminority faculty can also serve to reduce the sense of isolation. A Native village woman found great support from her white male instructors who provided individual attention and encouragement. This suggests the establishment of special, institutionalized mentoring relationships between university professors and students of color, a relationship that has shown positive results in other settings.[20] Another means of reducing isolation might be organizing students into cohorts, teams, or support groups. Such a structure may also help to reduce the negative repercussions of what has been called "token"[21] or "solo"[22] status, a condition occurring when a single individual is viewed as a representative of a low status group, often accompanied by assumptions of incompetence by majority culture members.

But there are larger problems at issue here, dilemmas not only for people of color but for all of us in teacher education specifically and for society in general: How can we structure education to encourage the active participation of students of color, and, for that matter, of all students? How can we best prepare our "mainstream" students to teach in the pluralistic society to which they will matriculate? How can we improve the education of the "minority" children who are likely to soon comprise the majority of children in our public schools? How can we lessen the "modern prejudice" that pervades our society, alienating and disempowering large segments of our population? I believe a reconceptualization of how we structure teacher education may provide the beginnings of a solution for all these issues.

The interviews quoted herein contain a gold mine of knowledge about how to educate not only teachers but *children* of color. From the interviewees' own learning experiences and from their knowledge of their own cultural backgrounds, they have developed models for educating children of their own cultural groups. Yet, judging from their reports, often this knowledge is barred from teacher education classes and not even formally explored with other teachers of the same culture. In short, we are, by virtue of our own pedagogical practices, excluding a great source of knowledge from our education curricula.

What might be the result if we restructure education classes so that all students are not merely allowed but *encouraged* to bring in their prior knowledge, their past experience, their own stories? The idea is not new. John Dewey advocated such a stance in 1904. In an article on the relationship between theory and practice in teacher education, he asserts that the "greatest asset in the student's possession – the greatest, moreover that ever will be in his possession – [is] his own direct and personal experience."[23]

Dewey recommends that students be encouraged to bring

their personal experiences to bear upon subject matter presented in the classroom. Doing otherwise, he warns, prevents teachers from developing and using their own independent intelligence and reinforces their "intellectual subserviency." Dewey further advises that failure to allow students to explore their past experiences in light of theoretical constructs will produce only a mindless imitation of others' practice rather than a reflection on teaching as an interactive process – and it will leave teachers prime targets for any educational publisher's grand, new, state-of-the-art magic potion.

This is indeed how the interviewees viewed the mindsets of their white colleagues when, as one teacher put it, these teachers seemed to be too book- or curriculum-bound, or, worse, "waiting for some program to ride in on a white horse and save them." It is interesting to note that although most teacher educators would heartily agree with the conceptions of good teaching espoused by these teachers of color, the teachers did not perceive their teacher education to have been based on such conceptions. Rather, they perceive teacher educators to be much like the classroom teachers they describe: whereas the classroom teachers are book- and curriculum-bound, the teacher educators "have never really been out there," but only go by "what they learned from books," or "only want to go by research they've read that other white people have written." In teacher education, "if you can't quote Vygotsky" then your words are not valid. If these teachers' perceptions are accurate, then Dewey's admonitions are doubly important to take to heart: not only might we not be allowing students to bring their critical intelligence to bear upon the teaching task, but we as teacher educators may be modeling behavior that is just the opposite of that which we wish to engender.

It seems likely that restructuring classes so as to build upon students' past experiences would appear to assist all potential teachers. Some teachers may need assistance in bringing reflection and critical thinking to the teaching role, thereby gaining encouragement to look beyond the books, the curriculum, and the experts to get in touch with their own "independent intelligence." Other teachers, particularly teachers of color, who may already have plenty of practice bringing their critical intelligence to bear upon the teaching task,[24] need to feel that their experiences and words are validated.

But the benefits of "story sharing" go beyond developing individual competencies or a sense of well-being. It is insufficient to allow students merely to make connections to their own pasts without exploring those pasts through multicultural lenses. Without such critical examination, we risk narrowing the student's perceptions and reducing his or her ability to understand diversity – so it is vitally important that the connections be examined, that the education professor highlight the narratives of the students of color and ask them to serve as resources for bringing to the fore differences in worldview, learning style, social organization, language, and so forth.

This could be accomplished by having small, culturally diverse teams of students observe children in classrooms, interview parents, or, through some other activity, collect data in order to develop potential strategies for working with diverse groups of children. The students should be encouraged to look to the "expert" in their group, the student or students from the same cultural group as the children observed, for advice and guidance in completing their assignments.[25]

This structuring effort can have several benefits. The educational problem posed by the professor is the group's to solve, but when a student of color is acknowledged as a source of valuable information, the group becomes dependent on his/her contributions. This can help to dispel any notions held by students (and faculty) about minority incompetence. Furthermore, during the informal interactions of the team members, common interests may become evident and possibly promote more interaction outside of the classroom across ethnic lines.[26] The students of color may find their experiences both admissible and valued in the classroom, which, along with the increased opportunity for interaction, may help to reduce their feelings of isolation from the university and their white classmates and professors.

On the other hand, white students will be encouraged to

search for solutions to educational problems rather than to depend on books and curriculum guides for answers. They will also gain valuable insight into people of color and ways of teaching diverse students, and learn ways to talk across differences in discourse styles and interactional patterns — lessons that will serve them well in their future teaching careers. In addition, all students will have gained a model for organizing their own classrooms. Several researchers have demonstrated that this structure is successful in encouraging full participation and student success in multicultural classrooms of younger students.[27]

Finally, organizing the university classroom so that all students' stories are heard and all opinions valued may make inroads into that persistent scourge of American society, racial prejudice and discrimination — "modern" or otherwise. As white students and faculty learn to listen to and respect the words of people of color, perhaps they will carry these new attitudes of openness and acceptance of difference to other aspects of their lives, and certainly to their future teaching. The interviews quoted herein are just an initial attempt to hear the voices of diversity represented in the field of education. They have much more to tell us.

Part 3

Looking to the Future: Accommodating Diversity

Looking to the Future:
Accommodating
Diversity

In the first two sections of this book I have described some of my thoughts on educating children of color, and have traced their origins through my experiences in this and other countries. I have proposed that in order to resolve the monumental problems we face in providing a quality education for poor children and children of color, we must open ourselves to learn from others with whom we may share little understanding.

Yet how do we use these insights to change what actually happens in the field of education? The path to accomplish this task is a long one; the essays in this section only begin to address the question.

The first essay, "Cross-cultural Confusions in Teacher Assessments," critiques some of the new teacher assessment models being designed in the present era of educational reform and offers some alternative approaches. Former models of assessment, primarily various forms of multiple choice tests, have been criticized as not capturing what teachers are actually able to do in the classroom. A version of this essay was originally presented to the staff of the Stanford Teacher Assessment Project (TAP) in 1987. The TAP grew out of a larger initiative to establish a National Board for Professional Teaching Standards (NBPTS). The idea behind the NBPTS is that, like doctors or lawyers, teachers should be certified nationally by a board governed by other teachers. The TAP staff, responsible for developing a prototype of a new kind of performance-based teacher assessment, had invited a group of scholars concerned about issues of cultural difference and equity to comment on the work of the project to date.

I had many concerns, particularly with a notion that seemed to permeate the project's work — that good teaching looked the same in any context or cultural setting. I was also concerned that the "one right way" philosophy would jeopardize the chances of teachers of color, or teachers of any ethnicity, who did not work in the settings the assessors were familiar with; in other words, those who worked in schools not populated by middle-class white children. The criticisms of the TAP project are just as valid for other new assessment schemes, from that of the Educational Testing Service, to the models now under design for the NBPTS. Just as students of different cultures may be unfairly judged by assessments designed for those from the "mainstream," teachers of different cultures may be equally handicapped.

I later developed my comments to that group into a paper presented at the 1988 Conference of the American Educational Research Association. Shortly thereafter, Sharon Nelson-Barber, a colleague of African-American and Native American ancestry, who worked on the TAP staff but held concerns similar to mine about the project, collaborated with me on yet another version of the paper. The version presented in this volume is a new combination of all of the previous papers.

The second essay, "The Politics of Teaching Literate Discourse," focuses on concerns that developed as a result of working with well-meaning liberal and even radical white teachers of English and language arts. Many teachers are reluctant to teach "standard English" to linguistically diverse students because they believe that to do so devalues the students' home languages. Further, these teachers have come to believe that, because of the interference of their students' home language and its emotional connection to their identities, the students would not be able to learn the "standard" form, even if it were taught.

This essay addresses my concern that such attitudes toward instruction handicap disenfranchised students, and then provides alternative ways to think about the problem. The first version of this paper was published in a special issue of Theory into Practice, *edited by Vivian Gadsden and devoted to literacy-related issues of access and equity.[1] The version presented here was originally published in the book* Freedom's Plow, *edited by James Fraser and Theresa Perry.*[2]

The final essay in this section, "Education in a Multicultural Society: Our Future's Greatest Challenge," is the slightly modified text of a speech presented at Howard University for their 1991 Charles H. Thompson lecture. I end with this piece because it summarizes much of what I believe needs to be changed to improve education for poor children and for children of color. If we are to succeed in this quest, we must recognize and address the power differentials that exist in our society between schools and communities, between teachers and parents, between poor and well-to-do, between whites and people of color. Further, we must understand that our view of the world is but one of many, that others see things in other ways.

During the writing of this book a small town in Alabama (two-thirds white and one-third black) was very much in the news. The white principal of the high school created a national stir when he threatened to cancel the prom because of interracial dating, and allegedly told a biracial student that her birth was "a mistake." There was a black boycott of the school, marches, demonstrations, and national calls for the principal's ouster. Six months after the alleged comments, the school was torched by the hands of an arsonist. The town was in shock.

What I found fascinating about the entire incident was not the principal's actions – there are always individuals in this country who are motivated by racial passions – but the different responses to the episode by black and white residents of the town. According to a news story[3] *covering the fire and the events which led up to it, the white population could not believe that their town could be at the heart of such a controversy. Those whites interviewed saw the principal of twenty-six years as a kind and fair man, one who helped out both black and white students. The black residents interviewed saw the principal in a completely different light. One commented dryly that sure, the principal helped a lot of black students out, he "helped them right out of the school." The article went on to report that the principal "is beloved by many whites, who see him as a wise disciplinarian. Yet he is apparently loathed by many blacks who say they have borne the brunt of his punishment."*

Even beyond the events surrounding the school incident, the community seemed distinctly divided. The white community believed there were no racial tensions in the town, a sentiment voiced by a prominent businessman and former teacher in the high school—"Do you see a problem? We get along in this town." Yet black residents claimed that the apparent calm was just a manifestation of the black community's having no power and no voice. In the words of a black minister, "If you walked into this town six months ago...you would have walked into 1950. You saw everyone get along well as long as you saw black people stay in their place." Two groups of people living side by side, smiling and greeting each other every morning and evening, yet, holding completely different views of the realities surrounding them — one group never conceiving of the other's sense of powerlessness and rage.

This combination of power and otherness is what this book is all about. Black, white, Indian, Hispanic or Asian, we must all find some way to come to terms with these two issues. When we teach across the boundaries of race, class, or gender — indeed when we teach at all — we must recognize and overcome the power differential, the stereotypes, and the other barriers which prevent us from seeing each other. Those efforts must drive our teacher education, our curriculum development, our instructional strategies, and every aspect of the educational enterprise. Until we can see the world as others see it, all the educational reforms in the world will come to naught.

Cross-cultural Confusions in Teacher Assessment

O ne of the most difficult tasks we face as human beings is trying to communicate across our individual differences, trying to make sure that what we say to someone is interpreted the way we intend. This becomes even more difficult when we attempt to communicate across social differences, gender, race, or class lines, or any situation of unequal power.

The assessment of teachers is a prime arena in which to examine these barriers to effective communication. Not only are teachers responsible for communicating to increasingly diverse students and their parents, but teachers themselves are a diverse lot whose assessment by examiners from other social groups can be fraught with serious misinterpretation. When intentions are misinterpreted, actions may be misinterpreted as well. As historian Jay Featherstone puts it, "If people read what you're doing entirely differently, then what you're doing will be entirely different."[1]

In recent years, much attention has been paid to the assessment and certification of teachers. New ways of looking at teaching, coupled with advances in measurement technology, have placed conventional tests and widely used observation procedures under close scrutiny by research groups, state licensure agencies, teacher education programs, and the test developers themselves. Research groups responding to the increasing national dissatisfaction with the quality of teacher testing include the Holmes Group; the now-completed Teacher Assessment Project (TAP), formerly housed at Stanford University; and more recently the Educational Testing Service, which has announced plans to replace the traditional National Teachers Examination with its own performance-based measures.

These efforts are attempting to establish technical and theoretical bases for the more realistic kind of teacher assessments called for by the recently formed National Board for Professional Teaching Standards. Central to the work of the board is the creation of a system of standards of excellence for classroom teachers that captures the knowledge and reasoning required in teaching as well as the uses to which that knowledge and reasoning are put.[2] This new attempt is promising because, in focusing on what teachers need to know and do in real classrooms, it is intended to minimize biases and to highlight strengths of culturally diverse teachers which might not be revealed through existing tests.

It is easy to assume, when we attempt to develop a fair and culturally sensitive means to assess teachers, that anything must be better than what we have typically used in the past – the National Teachers' Exam, a "fill in the blank" test much like the SAT or any other standardized test. However, this may not be the case. Those who are thoughtful and fair-minded have long understood that the traditional National Teachers' Exam is ethnically and culturally discriminatory, contributing to wholesale elimination of people of color from the teaching force. If a new assessment process is developed that purports to be sensitive to cultural differences, then the general expectation will be that this is indeed true. If, in actual practice, that assessment eliminates nonmainstream cultural groups at the same rate as previous "nonsensitive" assessments, then the general public can only conclude that something is wrong with teachers of color – for, after all, *these* assessments were designed to account for cultural differences.

Thus, the more "sophisticated" assessment can result in a situation worse than the status quo, one that creates even more negative stereotypical assumptions about the people of color it purports to help. My grave concern about this possibility leads me to pose the following issues for discussion among those who seek to create new assessment tools.

First, I'll offer an extended metaphor to clarify the concept of culturally influenced teaching styles. Reformers of educational policy have often looked to law, business, and medicine to develop models for improving the training and assessment of teachers. After trying to identify points of intersection between these professions, I've realized that teaching does not closely resemble any of them. The more I pondered their lack of similarity, the more I have been drawn to the resemblance of teaching to another profession – preaching. This may seem an unlikely comparison at first blush, but consider this: ministers are the only professionals who, like teachers, see their clients in a group. Further, they must not only present subject matter, but must also convince clients to incorporate that subject matter into their lives. In teaching as well as preaching, there are components of both content and motivation, of values and technique. Most intriguing about this particular comparison is the help it might provide in identifying cultural factors so sorely missing in current teacher assessment practices.

There are various styles of preaching. If the preacher's message is to be heard, however, it must relate to the cultural style of the constituencies being addressed. This is not the forum for an extended analysis of speech styles, but some examples quickly come to mind. The Southern black Baptist style is intricately connected to context, with a dependence on "paralinguistic" features. Rhythm, intonation, gesture, emotion, humor, use of metaphor, indirect personalized messages to individuals, and audience participation are crucial to communication in the black church, features which are but slightly modified reflections of secular black communication style.[3]

By contrast, I have had occasion to visit the services of a white Episcopalian minister in Harvard Square. As opposed to the context-boundedness of the black Baptist style, the Episcopalian style was syntactically bound: the meaning was to be found solely in the words, not in the context, the gestures or rhythm. The key to the sermon was logical structure rather than emotional tone or metaphorical allusions. Humor was the exception rather than the rule, and messages were directed to the entire congregation, never to individuals. These aspects of style are closely aligned with the middle-class, academic cultural style of this particular Cambridge, Massachusetts audience.[4]

Suppose we set out to evaluate and certify ministers nationally. What questions might we ask? A good start might be to question their knowledge of the subject matter; in this case, probably the scriptures. However, someone knowledgeable about scriptures but lacking the ability to communicate this knowledge to his congregation is not going to be successful at preaching, even less at moving the congregation to incorporate that knowledge into their daily lives. So we can say that subject matter knowledge is necessary, but insufficient.

If we attempt to move beyond assessing knowledge of subject matter, what could we do with the plethora of cultural styles of preaching? Can we try to evaluate, for example, Bishop Sheen, Billy Graham, and Reverend Ike (a Southern black Baptist minister) within the same conceptual construct? Or would we be better off asking what good preaching looks like in different cultural settings and for different audiences? After all, Bishop Sheen, would not be much of a hit in most black Baptist churches, and Reverend Ike would not be likely to impress the denizens of Harvard Square.

The issues of assessing teachers are analogous to the problems of assessing preachers. Whereas many thoughtful educators and educational researchers are in agreement that students are diverse in their culturally influenced learning styles, interactional patterns, and speech styles, there is much less discussion about culturally influenced differences among teachers. This diversity means that the actions of teachers who differ in worldview from those who seek to assess them can lead to misinterpretations about competence, quality, and intent.

Assessing diverse teachers becomes problematic in several ways, which can be categorized under two general headings: misinterpretations that occur at the level of the *practice of teaching* and those that occur in *talking about practice*.

Good teaching is not thought of in the same way in all communities. Just as what is considered to be good preaching in Harvard Square differs radically from the same in rural Georgia, beliefs about what constitutes good teaching vary across different cultural communities. Mainstream thinking holds that teaching begins with teachers' awareness of and ability to transfer knowledge. In an excellent explication of this position, Lee Shulman concludes, "Thus, teaching necessarily begins with a teacher's understanding of what is to be learned and how it is to be taught."[5] However, I have learned from interviews and personal experiences with teachers from communities of color that many of these individuals believe teaching begins instead with the establishment of relationships between themselves and their students.

In a 1989 interview, the exemplary teacher Jaime Escalante, widely known for his success with low-income Hispanic students in East Los Angeles (as chronicled in the movie *Stand and Deliver*), acknowledges his strong background in mathematics but insists that this alone does not account for his success. "Really, it's not just the knowledge of math.... My skills are really to motivate these kids to make them learn, to give them *ganas* – the desire to do something – to make them believe they can learn."[6]

Both perspectives include the three elements of teacher, student and content, but each provides for different relationships among the three. Perhaps the Shulman-reported model might be graphically represented like this,

TEACHER <----------> CONTENT <----------> STUDENT

where the content mediates the relationship between teacher and student. Teachers interact with content in order to help students interact with content. The other model might be portrayed like this,

where the strongest relationship is between student and teacher, with content only one aspect of their relationship.

Research suggests that children of color value the social aspects of an environment to a greater extent than do "mainstream" children, and tend to put an emphasis on feelings, acceptance, and emotional closeness. Research has also shown that motivation in African-American children from low socioeconomic groups is more influenced by the need for affiliation than for achievement.[7] Barbara Shade contends that African-American interpretations of the environment determine the amount and kind of effort students will expend on classroom tasks.[8] In a series of studies at the University of Alaska which sought to look at communication patterns and Native student retention, researchers found that the single characteristic that Native Alaskan students attributed to those professors they judged most positively was being "human." For these students, it was important to get a sense of the real human being playing the role of instructor.

While successful teachers of students of color may be responding to their students' real needs, that response may have negative consequences for the teachers' assessment. Clearly, all teachers must engage students and engage them with content as well; the issue is which of the two is considered more important. Teachers who view creating relationships between themselves and their students as central to the teaching task may be misjudged by assessors expecting to evaluate their knowledge of and involvement with content.

One instance of such misjudgment occurred in an exercise designed at Stanford University to devise teacher assessments in real classroom contexts. The assessment candidates were asked to teach a familiar lesson to a group of students brought together solely for that purpose. The candidates, for the most part from other parts of the country, had never met the students. An African-American teacher received poor marks for his lesson, which appeared scattered and illogical to the assessors. To one sensitive to alternative concepts of good teaching, however, it was clear that he was a teacher who believed it was necessary to establish a relationship with the students before then moving on to teach content. He appeared incompetent because he vacilated between trying to establish a rapport – to know and be known by the students – and attempting to teach the subject at hand.

Related to this sense of personal connectedness is a cultural difference in the level of emotional display considered appropriate in the teaching role. In mainstream educational thinking, teachers are often characterized as dispassionate arbiters of knowledge and tasks. Emotion can be viewed as counterproductive to rational scholarship and objectivity.[9] Furthermore, the belief that teachers who exhibit emotion must be "losing control" likely underlies the proliferation of methods of discipline that remove teacher affect from the classroom. For example, "management systems" such as "assertive discipline," "behavior modification," or "logical consequences" aim at discouraging displays of teacher emotion.[10]

Other cultural groups consider expressions of genuine emotion and personal presence to be at the core of the teaching role. A Native Alaskan graduate student shared this attitude in her personal account of an incident with her professor at a prestigious university. She had been having difficulty in the class because she did not understand many of the professor's points and felt too distanced from him/her to ask for clarification. Finally, in exasperation, she blurted out what amounted to, "This is supposed to be a class about communication and I don't understand a damn thing that's being said." The professor, looking equally chagrined, declared with frustration, "Well, I don't understand what the hell it is you don't understand!" For the student, this outburst was a relief – the professor had become a real person and was now approachable. She later commented with a chuckle, "Now that was a *real* person using *honest* words, and I can deal with that!"

According to a recent study exploring culturally influenced notions about good teaching within the African-American community:

> [Black] students grant teachers a wide latitude of emotions in which to make their expectations and dissatisfactions known. Assertive, aggressive and even angry behavior are all rated as acceptable means

of communicating one's intentions as long as these emotions are perceived as genuine. If expressions of emotion are too subtle, however, students are likely to misread a teacher's intentions and become disoriented. Responses lacking a sufficient emotional quality are likely to [be] read as non-caring. Totally unacceptable, however, is non-responsiveness. Students expect a response, and failing to get one will generally interpret this behavior as non-concern. From students' perspective the non-responsive teacher demonstrates not only lack of control, but a non-caring attitude as well.[11]

The consequences of such perceptions clearly play out in assessment situations where African-American teachers who display strong emotions are often viewed as too authoritarian, "pushy," and harsh with their students. Not surprisingly, these teachers frequently earn poor ratings. However, in many African-American communities, teachers are expected to show that they care about their students by controlling the class; exhibiting personal power; establishing meaningful interpersonal relationships; displaying emotion to garner student respect; demonstrating the belief that all students can learn; establishing a standard of achievement and "pushing" students to achieve the standard; and holding the attention of the students by incorporating African-American interactional styles in their teaching.[12] Teachers who do not exhibit these behaviors may be viewed by community members as ineffectual, boring, or uncaring.

African-American and Native American teachers may display emotions differently, but the assessment consequences are often the same. In schools in which the students are Native American and the majority of teachers and administrators are Anglo, Native teachers are often berated for "lacking a professional attitude." In both examples described below, the schools employed detailed management systems that all teachers and students were expected to honor. Unfortunately, these carefully laid plans did not take into account local norms about the handling of conflict, how respect is earned, or how discipline is maintained — eventually leading to many confusing situations for students and the unfair treatment of some of the Native teachers.

In the first example, a Native teacher stopped two students she found fighting in the hallway. Fully aware of the consequences of their actions, the students asked the teacher if she intended to tell the principal as mandated by school disciplinary policy. The teacher looked at the youngsters and bowed her head, saying, "I'd be ashamed to." The boys, greatly embarrassed by her remark, refrained from fighting for the remainder of the school year.

In this case, rather than acting in the role of dispassionate arbiter as dictated by the school, the teacher called upon her personal relationship with the students as a means of changing their behavior. In other words, rather than resorting to the power rooted in her role as a classroom teacher, she drew upon her sense of emotional affiliation with them. Whether or not the principal had knowledge of the cultural underpinnings of the teacher's actions, he characterized the teacher's failure to report the boys as "a major breach of professional conduct" because, in his estimation, abdicating the role of teacher amounted to placing the school's entire management system at risk. The fact that the boys' behavior had changed did not seem to matter.

In a second example, while proctoring the detention of a student who was expected to sit silently for one hour, a Native teacher instead discussed with the student the many accomplishments of his great-grandfather, whom the teacher had known as a great chief when she was young. She stressed what a wonderful, powerful leader he was and how he moved the entire village to do great things. Although she did not specifically mention the student's misbehavior, implicit in her message was the notion that a descendent of such a great man also possessed the qualities of a great leader. As the year progressed, the student needed only a look from the teacher or a reference to his great-grandfather to stifle any negative inclinations. As in the case above, the principal saw the situation very differently: passing by the detention classroom and noting a smile on the student's face, the principal chastised the teacher for talking to the student and for failing to reprimand him.

Each of these examples speaks to difficulties that can arise when perspectives differ — differences grounded in the values learned as an aspect of an individual's ethnic identity. If the administrators previously described were unable to interpret adequately what they were seeing, would performance-based assessors do any better? As we seek to develop new modes of assessment which move away from simplistic paper-and-pencil tests, we immediately face this dilemma. Yet we cannot presume to develop any assessment that will be fair and equitable unless great efforts are made to include the culturally influenced perspectives of diverse communities.

If, in the future, teachers will be expected not only to perform but to justify their actions during assessment interviews, no area will need to be understood more than the difficulties inherent in talking across cultures, ethnicities, and power differentials. What issues must assessors face if they are accurately to interpret the talk and actions of diverse teachers?

Just as cultural groups determine how their members view the world, so they determine how the world is talked about as well. As a consequence of each cultural group having developed its own particular communicative style, miscommunications in ethnically mixed conversations are numerous, including differences in how turns are taken in conversations, use of metaphor and indirect language, organization of talk, and more subtle features such as the rhythmic or tonal patterns of speech. Being able to make accurate interpretations requires either sharing communicative or ethnic background, or having enough communicative experience with the other group to make sense of the alternative styles. In an assessment setting, where a power differential exists between any assessor and teacher candidate, communicative style can be a significant factor in a candidate's success.

It might seem fairly straightforward to devise a series of questions for teachers which would tap the knowledge and reasoning that underlies their instruction. However, differences in how individuals and groups communicate can complicate this deceptively simple premise. For example,

members of middle-class academic culture tend to assume little shared knowledge among one another in formal settings
and expect to state explicitly all relevant information in order
to make their messages understood,[13] whereas other cultures
and classes maintain communicative ideals that consider it
unnecessary for speakers to state knowledge they presume to
share with one another – value is seldom placed on displaying
information for its own sake.[14] Stating the obvious or "saying
what everyone knows" is not encouraged; it is perceived as
"redundant," even insulting to the listener, and lacking communicative purpose.[15]

Similarly, in a study that analyzed the difficulties experienced by Japanese college students in a university-level speaking class, Alice Yan found that Japanese students had trouble
following the guidelines set by the teacher for giving a good
speech because they ran counter to Japanese cultural norms of
politeness. It was considered rude by these students to be too
explicit in developing a line of thinking that might include
information already known to the audience. Yan summarized
their reasoning as follows:

> Some of the students also mentioned that they did not think it was
> necessary to have an introduction because "everyone already knows
> that you are going to say something" and they will listen anyway.
> In addition, they mentioned that because people shared the same
> main information (i.e., cultural background), they did not want to
> say something too obvious or be too direct for fear of offending the
> audience.[16]

If this were an assessment situation, the teacher candidate
might, out of politeness, make a concerted effort not to talk
about "the obvious." However, the assessor might miscon-
strue this to mean that the candidate *did not know* the obvious.

Further complicating the issue, the narratives of some cultural groups take forms that are unfamiliar to Western academic culture, and as a consequence appear to be rambling and
without much point. There is a sizeable body of research
reporting that during the course of conversation many
African-Americans present information indirectly, through
use of metaphor or reference to presumably shared experience.

If listeners do not possess the background understanding needed to fill the gaps, accurate interpretation becomes a difficult task.[17] There is also a great deal of evidence to show that speakers from many Native American groups typically recount an event by offering a series of perspectives on a topic, with the expectation that the *listener* should take on the responsibility of supplying background information, relating subtopics, and making relevant judgments.[18] Western listeners, waiting for the speaker to "make the point," are often left confused by the conversation.

There are also differences across cultures as to how long a speaker should be allowed to speak at one turn, the length of pauses between turns, and how to get the floor for a turn. Researchers have identified such barriers to communication between several Native American groups and Anglo-Americans.[19] In brief, the Native Americans usually expect to take long speech turns, and once getting the floor they expect not to be interrupted until all their points are made. The problems arise in part because the two groups have different notions about how long a pause is appropriate during one's turn and how long is appropriate *between* turns.

According to researchers Ron and Suzanne Scollon, for example, the Athabaskan Indian's pause time *within* a turn is just long enough to make the Anglo think the Athabaskan has finished speaking.[20] The result is that the Athabaskan is left thinking that the Anglo is rudely interrupting, without allowing him or her to finish an idea. The Anglo-American is left believing that the Athabaskan doesn't make much sense and can't seem to express a complete idea. The implications of this mutual misunderstanding for an assessment situation should be obvious. Without knowledge about the cultural differences in timing and speech distribution within different groups, assessors may unduly and unintentionally penalize diverse teacher candidates.

Further, there are forms of assessment data gathering that could unduly penalize candidates from cultural groups different from that of the assessors. One particular strategy might be labeled, "On the folly of asking *A* when you're really trying to find out *B.*" Assessment questions that ask one thing while using the response to determine knowledge of something else are blatantly unfair. Candidates who are members of the assessor's cultural group and who also tend toward volubility are likely to be rated higher under such circumstances. This is not because they know more, but because their comembership makes "reading between the lines" easier, and their very volubility makes eventually hitting upon an appropriate response to an unasked question more likely.

As an example, in the "Teaching a Familiar Lesson" assessment prototype of the Stanford Teacher Assessment Project, candidates were required to teach a group of students a lesson in history and then respond to such questions as, "What are your feelings about how the class went?", "Did you have to make any significant adaptations or changes to your plan?", "How well did the students get the point of the lesson?", and "What should tomorrow's lesson be?"[21] The responses, however, were rated against the following criteria: whether the candidate "identifie[d] learning objectives for lessons described and [gave] justification of why chosen teaching method...[was] effective," "discuss[ed] history as ongoing contributor to students' lives," and "[made] reference to strengths and weaknesses of own teaching."[22] By not informing candidates about what is really being measured, assessors are likely to unfairly penalize some culturally different candidates.

In some cultures, what gets said is a function of the person to whom one is speaking. In Athabaskan communities, for example, it is expected that the individual with a higher status role (which would be the assessor in an assessment setting) will speak most. The subordinate participant is expected to take the role of spectator, to learn by watching and listening. This difference in the expected conversational roles can create havoc in an assessment setting in which the assessor is expecting the candidate to speak freely about his or her work.

In academic, middle-class culture, the relationship between speaker and listener is deemphasized, and the content of the message is of primary importance. Here speakers are expected to lay out information in a linear fashion, provide background information, and guide the listener to specific conclusions.[23] Assessors accustomed to this style are likely to suspect that seemingly indirect, highly contextualized, or reticent responses suggest that the candidate does not have an answer to a question. Because they believe they will not be hearing the information requested, they are likely to interrupt the response in midstream and, as a consequence, prevent the candidate from demonstrating competence.

A further complication is that teachers from some cultures do not expect to have to show competence by *talking* about what they do. They expect that anyone wanting to know what they do in a classroom will watch them teach and then make judgments about their competence. From the perspective of many Native American teachers, the doing of a task should be evidence of competence, whereas Western academic culture views competence as being evidenced only in *talking* about what one has done. Teachers from some cultural groups will likely be reluctant in an interview setting to *talk* about what they may be very good at *doing* – and the assessor may assume, then, that the candidate is incapable of doing what he or she can't explain.

Assessors also need to understand that some cultural groups perform more effectively when assessment is conducted in "authentic" situations, so that the goal of talk is to actually provide new information to the assessor. I observed an Athabaskan Indian teacher education student in an assessment setting in which he was to teach to his professors and classmates, who were assigned the role of second graders, a lesson on everyday items that sink or float. He apparently found this decontextualized, inauthentic task very frustrating, and changed – abruptly and without explanation – to a lesson about the culture of his community. He changed the communicative task from a contrived test setting to a realistic encounter in which he provided new information to his classmates and professors. Fortunately, I was a faculty member at the student's institution. When I recognized what was happening, I was able to intervene when others in the group wanted to give this student a poor grade. After a thorough discussion, the group finally agreed that there was an innate unfairness in judging performances rooted in one set of norms against the very different and unstated set of norms most of the faculty in the room took for granted. The fact that these kinds of discussions are beginning to take place in schools of education shows promise that the perspectives of more poor and minority groups' members will be heard.

It is important to be clear about the following point. Although I make the case that norms of communication vary across groups, I do not mean to imply that it would be unreasonable to ask teacher candidates to explain what they do in the classroom and why. The problem lies not in asking teachers to explain their teaching but in recognizing that in diverse communities there may be differences in what it *means* to explain one's teaching. Such differences in conventionalized expectation about what counts as an appropriate response work to the disadvantage of some speakers. If new, broad standards are to be devised, the criteria for an exemplary performance must be made explicit so that schools of education can ensure that all students understand those criteria. Although some students might have to make additional efforts to learn new ways of exhibiting competence, candidates would at least know from the beginning what standard they are being judged against.

One way to eliminate some of the difficulties implicit in the examples cited above would be to provide opportunities for candidates to talk in real contexts. Instead of asking teachers only to talk about their teaching to assessors to whom they are likely to be particularly indirect – because they do not wish to insult assessors by stating the obvious, or because they feel uncomfortable talking in a contrived setting – teachers can be observed instead mentoring or supervising student teachers. In such authentic settings, the candidate would likely be more direct and explicit, as prior knowledge would not be assumed in a novice. The teacher's actual competence might be better exhibited. Of couse, such an approach would require that some pool of evaluators be equipped to recognize

culturally appropriate responses and not conclude that difference implies inadequacy.

Although mainstream U.S. society assumes that candidates in
an assessment setting will strive to present themselves in the
best possible light, the methods used to display one's
strengths, as we have seen, vary from group to group. An
activity as taken for granted as talking about one's accomplishments may be considered inappropriate or in poor taste
for cultural groups that maintain strong prohibitions against
appearing boastful. In some Asian and Native American cultures, for example, positive evaluations must be made by
someone else.[24]

As a case in point, I once tried to help an Aleut woman in
completing graduate school applications. Although Martha
had extensive experience in many areas and was skilled academically, she had not specified these talents (even after several
drafts and much encouragement) in her personal statement.
After much insistence that this information would strengthen
her application, she stated, aghast, "But then my elders will
say, 'Now no one has to praise you!'" In other words, speaking
about her own accomplishments was the ultimate expression
of arrogance. Due to the depth of her feelings, an alternative
plan was devised in which she used her personal statement to
discuss issues she felt comfortable addressing, including her
tribe's cultural prohibitions against exhibitionism. I wrote a
separate letter detailing her many accomplishments.

Since many candidates are often reluctant to speak on their
own behalf, then, assessment contexts might require advocates familiar enough with an individual's work to attest to
their skills and abilities.

Another major area of concern in cross-cultural assessment
lies in the sociopolitical realities of interracial interaction in
this country. Researchers have found that there are a number
of ways in which people of color are discriminated against in
interview settings. While it will be difficult to find solutions
to this problem, one possibility might be to allow teacher

candidates some role in the selection of their examiners. Perhaps the candidate could be given a list of approved examiners from which to choose at least one. At the very least, attention must be paid to the issue of discrimination and bias in the selection and training of evaluators.

Although here I could neither fully explore nor offer solutions to all the problems of assessing teachers from different cultural groups, I do believe that the best solutions will arise from the acceptance that alternative worldviews exist – that there are valid alternative means to any end, as well as valid alternative ends in themselves. We all interpret behaviors, information, and situations through our own cultural lenses; these lenses operate involuntarily, below the level of conscious awareness, making it seem that our own view is simply "the way it is." Learning to interpret across cultures demands reflecting on our own experiences, analyzing our own culture, examining and comparing varying perspectives. We must consciously and voluntarily make our cultural lenses apparent. Engaging in the hard work of seeing the world as others see it must be a fundamental goal for any move to reform the education of teachers and their assessment.

The Politics of Teaching Literate Discourse

I have encountered a certain sense of powerlessness and paralysis among many sensitive and well-meaning literacy educators who appear to be caught in the throes of a dilemma. Although their job is to teach literate discourse styles to all of their students, they question whether that is a task they can actually accomplish for poor students and students of color. Furthermore, they question whether they are acting as agents of oppression by insisting that students who are not already a part of the "mainstream" learn that discourse. Does it not smack of racism or classism to demand that these students put aside the language of their homes and communities and adopt a discourse that is not only alien, but that has often been instrumental in furthering their oppression? I hope here to speak to and help dispel that sense of paralysis and powerlessness and suggest a path of commitment and action that not only frees teachers to teach what they know, but to do so in a way that can transform and subsequently liberate their students.

DISCOURSE, LITERACY, AND GEE

This article got its start as I pondered the dilemmas expressed by educators. It continued to evolve when a colleague sent a set of papers to me for comment. The papers, authored by literacy specialist James Paul Gee ("Literacy, Discourse, and Linguistics: Introduction" and "What Is Literacy?"), are the lead articles of a special issue of the *Journal of Education*[1] devoted solely to Gee's work. The papers brought to mind many of the perspectives of the educators I describe. My colleague, an academic with an interest in literacy issues in communities of color, was disturbed by much of what she read in the articles and wanted a second opinion.

As I first read the far-reaching, politically sensitive articles, I found that I agreed with much that Gee wrote, as I have with much of his previous work. He argues that literacy is much more than reading and writing, but rather that it is part of a larger political entity. This larger entity he calls a discourse, construed as something of an "identity kit," that is, ways of "saying–writing–doing–being–valuing–believing," examples of which might be the discourse of lawyers, the discourse of academics, or the discourse of men. He adds that one never learns simply to read or write, but to read and write within some larger discourse, and therefore within some larger set of values and beliefs.

Gee maintains that there are primary discourses, those learned in the home, and secondary discourses, which are attached to institutions or groups one might later encounter. He also argues that all discourses are not equal in status, that some are socially dominant – carrying with them social power and access to economic success – and some nondominant. The status of individuals born into a particular discourse tends to be maintained because primary discourses are related to secondary discourses of similar status in our society (for example, the middle-class home discourse to school discourse, or the working-class African-American home discourse to the black church discourse). Status is also maintained because dominant groups in a society apply frequent "tests" of fluency in the dominant discourses, often focused on its most superficial aspects – grammar, style, mechanics – so as to exclude from full participation those who are not born to positions of power.

These arguments resonate in many ways with what I also believe to be true. However, as I reread and pondered the articles, I began to get a sense of my colleague's discomfort. I also began to understand how that discomfort related to some concerns I have about the perspectives of educators who sincerely hope to help educate poor children and children of color to become successful and literate, but who find themselves paralyzed by their own conception of the task.

There are two aspects of Gee's arguments which I find problematic. First is Gee's notion that people who have not been born into dominant discourses will find it exceedingly difficult, if not impossible, to acquire such a discourse. He argues strongly that discourses cannot be "overtly" taught, particularly in a classroom, but can only be acquired by enculturation in the home or by "apprenticeship" into social practices. Those who wish to gain access to the goods and status connected to a dominant discourse must have access to the social practices related to that discourse. That is, to learn the "rules" required for admission into a particular dominant discourse, individuals must already have access to the social institutions connected to that discourse – if you're not already in, don't expect to get in.

This argument is one of the issues that concerned my colleague. As she put it, Gee's argument suggests a dangerous kind of determinism as flagrant as that espoused by the geneticists: instead of being locked into "your place" by your genes, you are now locked hopelessly into a lower-class status by your discourse. Clearly, such a stance can leave a teacher feeling powerless to effect change, and a student feeling hopeless that change can occur.

The second aspect of Gee's work that I find troubling suggests that an individual who is born into one discourse with one set of values may experience major conflicts when attempting to acquire another discourse with another set of values. Gee defines this as especially pertinent to "women and minorities," who, when they seek to acquire status discourses, may be faced with adopting values that deny their primary identities. When teachers believe that this acceptance of self-deprecatory values is *inevitable* in order for people of color to acquire status discourses, then their sense of justice and fair play might hinder their teaching these discourses.

If teachers were to adopt both of these premises suggested

by Gee's work, not only would they view the acquisition of a new discourse in a classroom impossible to achieve, but they might also view the goal of acquiring such a discourse questionable at best. The sensitive teacher might well conclude that even to try to teach a dominant discourse to students who are members of a nondominant oppressed group would be to oppress them further. And this potential conclusion concerns me. While I do agree that discourses may embody conflicting values, I also believe there are many individuals who have faced and overcome the problems that such a conflict might cause. I hope to provide another perspective on both of these premises.

OVERCOMING OBSTACLES TO ACQUISITION

One remedy to the paralysis suffered by many teachers is to bring to the fore stories of the real people whose histories directly challenge unproductive beliefs. Mike Rose has done a poignantly convincing job of detailing the role of committed teachers in his own journey toward accessing literate discourse, and his own role as a teacher of disenfranchised veterans who desperately needed the kind of explicit and focused instruction Rose was able to provide in order to "make it" in an alien academic setting.[2] But there are many stories not yet documented which exemplify similar journeys, supported by similar teaching.

A friend and colleague who teaches in a college of education at a major Midwestern university, told me of one of her graduate students whom we'll call Marge. Marge received a special fellowship funded by a private foundation designed to increase the numbers of faculty holding doctorates at black colleges. She applied to the doctoral program at my friend's university and traveled to the institution to take a few classes while awaiting the decision. Apparently, the admissions committee did not quite know what to do with her, for here was someone who was already on campus with a fellowship, but who, based on GRE scores and writing samples, they determined was not capable of doing doctoral-level work. Finally,

the committee agreed to admit Marge into the master's program, even though she already held a master's degree. Marge
accepted the offer. My friend – we'll call her Susan – got to
know Marge when the department head asked her to "work
with" the new student who was considered "at risk" of not
successfully completing the degree.

Susan began a program to help Marge learn how to cope
with the academic setting. Susan recognized early on that
Marge was very talented but that she did not understand how
to maneuver her way through academic writing, reading, and
talking. In their first encounters, Susan and Marge discussed
the comments instructors had written on Marge's papers,
and how the next paper might incorporate the professor's
concerns. The next summer Susan had Marge write weekly
synopses of articles related to educational issues. When
they met, Marge talked through her ideas while Susan
took notes. Together they translated the ideas into the "discourse of teacher education." Marge then rewrote the papers
referring to their conversations and Susan's extensive written
comments.

Susan continued to work with Marge, both in and out of
the classroom, during the following year. By the end of that
year, Marge's instructors began telling Susan that Marge was a
real star, that she had written the best papers in their classes.
When faculty got funding for various projects, she became
one of the most sought-after research assistants in the college.
And when she applied for entry into the doctoral program the
next fall, even though her GRE scores were still low, she was
accepted with no hesitation. Her work now includes research
and writing that challenge dominant attitudes about the
potential of poor children to achieve.

The stories of two successful African-American men also
challenge the belief that literate discourses cannot be acquired
in classroom settings, and highlight the significance of teachers in transforming students' futures. Clarence Cunningham,
now a vice chancellor at the largest historically black institution in the United States, grew up in a painfully poor community in rural Illinois. He attended an all–African-American

elementary school in the 1930s in a community where the parents of most of the children never even considered attending high school. There is a school picture hanging in his den of a ragtag group of about thirty-five children. As he shows me that picture, he talks about the one boy who grew up to be a principal in Philadelphia, one who is now a vice president of a major computer company, one who was recently elected attorney general of Chicago, another who is a vice president of Harris Bank in Chicago, another who was the first black pilot hired by a major airline. He points to a little girl who is now an administrator, another who is a union leader. Almost all of the children in the photo eventually left their home community, and almost all achieved impressive goals in life.

Another colleague and friend, Bill Trent, a professor and researcher at a major research university, told me of growing up in the 1940s and 1950s in inner-city Richmond, Virginia, "the capital of the Confederacy." His father, a cook, earned an eighth-grade education by going to night school. His mother, a domestic, had a third-grade education. Neither he nor his classmates had aspirations beyond their immediate environment. Yet, many of these students completed college, and almost all were successful, many notable. Among them are teachers, ministers, an electronics wizard, state officials, career army officers, tennis ace Arthur Ashe, and the brothers Max and Randall Robinson, the national newscaster and the director of Trans-Africa, respectively.

How do these men explain the transformations that occurred in their own and their classmates' lives? Both attribute their ability to transcend the circumstances into which they were born directly to their teachers. First, their teachers successfully taught what Gee calls the "superficial features" of middle-class discourse – grammar, style, mechanics – features that Gee claims are particularly resistant to classroom instruction. And the students successfully learned them.

These teachers also successfully taught the more subtle aspects of dominant discourse. According to both Trent and Cunningham, their teachers insisted that students be able to speak and write eloquently, maintain neatness, think carefully, exude character, and conduct themselves with decorum. They even found ways to mediate class differences by attending to the hygiene of students who needed such attention – washing faces, cutting fingernails, and handing out deodorant.

Perhaps more significant than what they taught is what they believed. As Trent says, "They held visions of us that we could not imagine for ourselves. And they held those visions even when they themselves were denied entry into the larger white world. They were determined that, despite all odds, we would achieve." In an era of overt racism when much was denied to African-Americans, the message drilled into students was "the one thing people can't take away from you is what's between your ears." The teachers of both men insisted that they must achieve because "you must do twice as well as white people to be considered half as good."

As Cunningham says, "Those teachers pushed us, they wouldn't let us fail. They'd say, 'The world is tough out there, and you have to be tougher.'" Trent recalls that growing up in the "inner-city," he had no conception of life beyond high school, but his high school teachers helped him to envision one. While he happily maintained a C average, putting all of his energy into playing football, he experienced a turning point one day when his coach called him inside in the middle of a practice. There, while he was still suited up for football, all of his teachers gathered to explain to him that if he thought he could continue making Cs and stay on the team he had another thing coming. They were there to tell him that if he did not get his act together and make the grades they knew he was capable of, then his football career would be over.

Like similar teachers chronicled elsewhere, these teachers put in overtime to ensure that the students were able to live up to their expectations. They set high standards and then carefully and explicitly instructed students in how to meet them. "You can and will do well," they insisted, as they taught at break times, after school, and on weekends to ensure that their students met their expectations. All of these teachers were able to teach in classrooms the rules for dominant discourses, allowing students to succeed in mainstream America who were not only born outside of the realms of power and status, but who had no access to status institutions. These teachers were not themselves a part of the power elite, not members of dominant discourses. Yet they were able to provide the keys for their students' entry into the larger world, never knowing if the doors would ever swing open to allow them in.

The renowned African-American sociologist E. Franklin Frazier also successfully acquired a discourse into which he was not born. Born in poverty to unschooled parents, Frazier learned to want to learn from his teachers and from his self-taught father. He learned his lessons so well that his achievements provided what must be the ultimate proof of the ability to acquire a secondary dominant discourse, no matter what one's beginnings. After Frazier completed his master's degree at Clark University, he went on to challenge many aspects of the white-dominated oppressive system of segregation. Ironically, at the time Frazier graduated from Clark, he received a reference from its president, G. Stanley Hall, who gave Frazier what he must have thought was the highest praise possible in a predominantly white university in 1920. "Mr. Frazier... seems to me to be quite gentlemanly and *mentally white.*"[3] What better evidence of Frazier's having successfully acquired the dominant discourse of academe?

These stories are of commitment and transformation. They show how people, given the proper support, can "make it" in culturally alien environments. They make clear that standardized test scores have little to say about one's actual ability. And they demonstrate that supporting students' transformation demands an extraordinary amount of time and commitment, but that teachers *can* make a difference if they are willing to make that commitment.

Despite the difficulty entailed in the process, almost any African-American or other disenfranchised individual who has become "successful" has done so by acquiring a discourse other than the one into which he or she was born. And almost all can attribute that acquisition to what happened as a result of the work of one or more committed teachers.

ACQUISITION AND TRANSFORMATION

But the issue is not only whether students can learn a dominant secondary discourse in the classroom. Perhaps the more significant issue is, should they attempt to do so? Gee contends that for those who have been barred from the mainstream, "acquisition of many mainstream Discourses...involves active complicity with the values that conflict with one's home and community-based Discourses." There can be no doubt that in many classrooms students of color do reject literacy, for they feel that literate discourses reject them. Keith Gilyard, in his jolting autobiographical study of language competence, graphically details his attempt to achieve in schools that denied the very existence of his community reality:

> I was torn between institutions, between value systems. At times the tug of school was greater, therefore the 90.2 average. On the other occasions the streets were a more powerful lure, thus the heroin and the 40 in English and a brief visit to the Adolescent Remand Shelter. I...saw no middle ground or more accurately, no total ground on which anomalies like me could gather. I tried to be a hip schoolboy, but it was impossible to achieve that persona. In the group I most loved, to be fully hip meant to repudiate a school system in which African-American consciousness was undervalued or ignored; in which, in spite of the many nightmares around us, I was urged to keep my mind on the Dream, to play the fortunate token, to keep my head straight down and "make it." And I pumped more and more dope into my arms. It was a nearly fatal response, but an almost inevitable one.[4]

Herb Kohl writes powerfully about individuals, young and old, who choose to "not-learn" what is expected of them rather than to learn that which denies them their sense of who they are:

> Not-learning tends to take place when someone has to deal with unavoidable challenges to her or his personal and family loyalties, integrity, and identity. In such situations there are forced choices

and no apparent middle ground. To agree to learn from a stranger who does not respect your integrity causes a major loss of self. The only alternative is to not-learn and reject the stranger's world.[5]

I have met many radical or progressive teachers of literacy who attempt to resolve the problem of students who choose to "not-learn" by essentially deciding to "not-teach." They appear to believe that to remain true to their ideology, their role must be to empower and politicize their most disenfranchised students by refusing to teach what Gee calls the superficial features (grammar, form, style, and so forth) of dominant discourses.[6] Believing themselves to be contributing to their students' liberation by deemphasizing dominant discourses, they instead seek to develop literacy *solely* within the language and style of the students' home discourse.

Feminist writer bell hooks writes of one of the consequences of this teaching methodology. During much of her postsecondary school career she was the only black student in her writing courses. Whenever she would write a poem in black Southern dialect, the teachers and fellow students would praise her for using her "true authentic voice" and encourage her to write more in this voice.[7] hooks writes of her frustration with these teachers who, like the teachers I describe, did not recognize the need for African-American students to have access to many voices and who maintained their stance even when adult students or the parents of younger students demanded that they do otherwise.

I am reminded of one educator of adult African-American veterans who insisted that her students needed to develop their "own voices" by developing "fluency" in their home language. Her students vociferously objected, demanding that they be taught grammar, punctuation, and "Standard English." The teacher insisted that such a mode of study was "oppressive." The students continued venting their objections in loud and certain tones. When asked why she thought her students had not developed "voice" when they were using their voices to loudly express their displeasure, she responded that it was "because of who they are," that is, apparently because they were working-class, black, and disagreed with her. Another educator of adults told me that she based her teaching on liberating principles. She voiced her anger with her mostly poor, working-class students because they rejected her pedagogy and "refused to be liberated." There are many such stories to recount.[8]

There are several reasons why students and parents of color take a position that differs from the well-intentioned position of the teachers I have described. First, they know that members of society need access to dominant discourses to (legally) have access to economic power. Second, they know that such discourses can be and have been acquired in classrooms because they know individuals who have done so. And third, and most significant to the point I wish to make now, they know that individuals have the ability to transform dominant discourses for liberatory purposes – to engage in what Henry Louis Gates calls "changing the joke and slipping the yoke,"[9] that is, using European philosophical and critical standards to challenge the tenets of European belief systems.

bell hooks speaks of her black women teachers in the segregated South as being the model from which she acquired both access to dominant discourses and a sense of the validity of the primary discourse of working-class African-American people. From their instruction, she learned that black poets were capable of speaking in many voices, that the Dunbar who wrote in dialect was as valid as the Dunbar who wrote sonnets. She also learned from these women that she was capable of not only participating in the mainstream, but redirecting its currents: "Their work was truly education for critical consciousness....They were the teachers who conceptualized oppositional world views, who taught us young black women to exult and glory in the power and beauty of our intellect. They offered to us a legacy of liberatory pedagogy that demanded active resistance and rebellion against sexism and racism."[10]

Carter G. Woodson called for similar pedagogy almost seventy years ago. He extolled teachers in his 1933 *Mis-Education of the Negro* to teach African-American students not only the language and canon of the European "mainstream," but to teach as well the life, history, language, philosophy, and literature of their own people. Only this kind of education, he argued, would prepare an educated class which would serve the needs of the African-American community.

Acquiring the ability to function in a dominant discourse need not mean that one must reject one's home identity and values, for discourses are not static, but are shaped, however reluctantly, by those who participate within them and by the form of their participation. Many who have played significant roles in fighting for the liberation of people of color have done so through the language of dominant discourses, from Frederick Douglass to Ida B. Wells, to Mary McCloud Bethune, to Martin Luther King, to Malcolm X. As did bell hooks' teachers, today's teachers can help economically disenfranchised students and students of color, both to master the dominant discourses and to transform them. How is the teacher to accomplish this? I suggest several possibilities.

What can teachers do? First, teachers must acknowledge and validate students' home language without using it to limit students' potential. Students' home discourses are vital to their perception of self and sense of community connectedness. One Native American college student I know says he cannot write in Standard English when he writes about his village "because that's about me!" Then he must use his own "village English" or his voice rings hollow even to himself. June Jordan has written a powerful essay about teaching a course in Black English and the class's decision to write a letter of protest in that language when the brother of one of the students was killed by police.[11] The point must not be to eliminate students' home languages, but rather to add other voices and discourses to their repertoires. As bell hooks and Henry Gates have poignantly reminded us, racism and oppression must be fought on as many fronts and in as many voices as we can muster.[12]

Second, teachers must recognize the conflict Gee details between students' home discourses and the discourse of school. They must understand that students who appear to be unable to learn are in many instances choosing to "not-learn" as Kohl puts it, choosing to maintain their sense of identity in the face of what they perceive as a painful choice between allegiance to "them" or "us." The teacher, however, can reduce this sense of choice by transforming the new discourse so that it contains within it a place for the students' selves. To do so, they must saturate the dominant discourse with new meanings, must wrest from it a place for the glorification of their students and their forbears.

An interesting historical example is documented by James Anderson. Anderson writes of Richard Wright, an African-American educator in the post-Reconstruction era, who found a way through the study of the "classical" curriculum to claim a place of intellectual respect for himself and his people. When examined by the U.S. Senate Committee on Education and Labor, one senator questioned Wright about the comparative inferiority and superiority of the races. Wright replied:

> It is generally admitted that religion has been a great means of human development and progress, and I think that about all the great religions which have blessed this world have come from the colored races – all...I believe, too, that our methods of alphabetic writing all came from the colored race, and I think the majority of the sciences in their origin have come from the colored races....Now I take the testimony of those people who know, and who, I feel are capable of instructing me on this point, and I find them saying that the Egyptians were actually wooly-haired negroes. In Humboldt's Cosmos (Vol. 2, p. 531) you will find that testimony, and Humboldt, I presume, is a pretty good authority. The same thing is stated in Herodotus, and in a number of other authors with whom you gentlemen are doubtless familiar. Now if that is true, the idea that the negro race is inherently inferior, seems to me to be at least a little limping.[13]

Noted educator Jaime Escalante prepared poor Latino students to pass the tests for advanced calculus when everyone else thought they would do well to master fractions. To do so, he also transformed a discourse by placing his students and their ancestors firmly within its boundaries. In a line from the movie chronicling his success, *Stand and Deliver,* he entreated his students, "You *have* to learn math. The Mayans discovered zero. Math is in your blood!"

And this is also what those who create what has been called "Afrocentric" curricula do. They too seek to illuminate for students (and their teachers) a world in which people with brown and black skin have achieved greatness and have developed a large part of what is considered the great classical tradition. They also seek to teach students about those who have taken the language born in Europe and transformed it into an emancipatory tool for those facing oppression in the "new world." In the mouths and pens of Bill Trent, Clarence Cunningham, bell hooks, Henry Louis Gates, Paul Lawrence Dunbar, and countless others, the "language of the master" has been used for liberatory ends. Students can learn of that rich legacy, and they can also learn that they are its inheritors and rightful heirs.

A final role that teachers can take is to acknowledge the unfair "discourse-stacking" that our society engages in. They can discuss openly the injustices of allowing certain people to succeed, based not upon merit but upon which family they were born into, upon which discourse they had access to as children. The students, of course, already know this, but the open acknowledgment of it in the very institution that facilitates the sorting process is liberating in itself. In short, teachers must allow discussions of oppression to become a part of language and literature instruction. Only after acknowledging the inequity of the system can the teacher's stance then be "Let me show you how to cheat!" And of course, to cheat is to learn the discourse which would otherwise be used to exclude them from participating in and transforming the mainstream. This is what many black teachers of the segregated South intended when they, like the teachers of Bill Trent and Clarence Cunningham, told their students that they *had* to "do better than those white kids." We can again let our students know that they can resist a system that seeks to limit them to the bottom rung of the social and economic ladder.

Gee may not agree with my analysis of his work, for, in truth, his writings are so multifaceted as not to be easily reduced to simplistic positions. But that is not the issue. The point is that some aspects of his work can be disturbing for the

African-American reader, and reinforcing for those who choose – wrongly, but for "right" reasons – not to educate black and poor children.

Individuals *can* learn the "superficial features" of dominant discourses, as well as their more subtle aspects. Such acquisition can provide a way both to turn the sorting system on its head and to make available one more voice for resisting and reshaping an oppressive system. This is the alternative perspective I want to give to teachers of poor children and children of color, and this is the perspective I hope will end the paralysis and set teachers free to teach, and thereby to liberate. When teachers are committed to teaching all students, and when they understand that through their teaching change *can* occur, then the chance for transformation is great.

Education in a Multicultural Society: Our Future's Greatest Challenge*

In any discussion of education and culture, it is important to remember that children are individuals and cannot be made to fit into any preconceived mold of how they are "supposed" to act. The question is not necessarily how to create the perfect "culturally matched" learning situation for each ethnic group, but rather how to recognize when there is a problem for a particular child and how to seek its cause in the most broadly conceived fashion. Knowledge about culture is but one tool that educators may make use of when devising solutions for a school's difficulty in educating diverse children.

THE CULTURAL CLASH BETWEEN STUDENTS AND SCHOOL

The clash between school culture and home culture is actualized in at least two ways. When a significant difference exists between the students' culture and the school's culture, teachers can easily misread students' aptitudes, intent, or abilities as a result of the difference in styles of language use and interactional patterns. Secondly, when such cultural differences exist, teachers may utilize styles of instruction and/or discipline that are at odds with community norms. A few examples: A twelve-year-old friend tells me that there are three kinds of teachers in his middle school: the black teachers, none of whom are afraid of black kids; the white teachers, a

*Presented at the 12th annual Charles H. Thompson Lecture – Colloquium, November 6, 1991. The speech has been slightly modified for publication.

few of whom are not afraid of black kids; and the largest group of white teachers, who are *all* afraid of black kids. It is this last group that, according to my young informant, consistently has the most difficulty with teaching and whose students have the most difficulty with learning.

I would like to suggest that some of the problems may certainly be as this young man relates. Yet, from my work with teachers in many settings, I have come to believe that a major portion of the problem may also rest with how these three groups of teachers interact and use language with their students. These differences in discourse styles relate to certain ethnic and class groups. For instance, many African-American teachers are likely to give directives to a group of unruly students in a direct and explicit fashion, for example, "I don't want to hear it. Sit down, be quiet, and finish your work NOW!" Not only is this directive explicit, but with it the teacher also displays a high degree of personal power in the classroom. By contrast, many middle-class European-American teachers are likely to say something like, "Would you like to sit down now and finish your paper?", making use of an indirect command and downplaying the display of power. Partly because the first instance is likely to be more like the statements many African-American children hear at home, and partly because the second statement sounds to many of these youngsters like the words of someone who is fearful (and thus less deserving of respect), African-American children are more likely to obey the first explicit directive and ignore the second implied directive.

The discussion of this issue is complex, but, in brief, many of the difficulties teachers encounter with children who are different in background from themselves are related to this underlying attitudinal difference in the appropriate display of explicitness and personal power in the classroom.

If teachers are to teach effectively, recognition of the importance of student perception of teacher intent is critical. Problems arising from culturally different interactional styles seem to disproportionately affect African-American boys, who, as a result of cultural influences, exhibit a high degree of physicality and desire for interaction. This can be expressed both positively and negatively, as hugging and other shows of affection or as hitting and other displays of displeasure. Either expression is likely to receive negative sanction in the classroom setting.

Researcher Harry Morgan documents in a 1990 study what most of us who have worked with African-American children have learned intuitively: that African-American children, more than white, and boys more than girls, initiate interactions with peers in the classroom in performing assigned tasks. Morgan concludes that a classroom that allows for greater movement and interaction will better facilitate the learning and social styles of African-American boys, while one that disallows such activity will unduly penalize them. This, I believe, is one of the reasons that there recently has been such a movement toward developing schools specifically for African-American males. Black boys *are* unduly penalized in our regular classrooms. They *are* disproportionately assigned to special education. They do not have to be, and would not be, if our teachers were taught how to redesign classrooms so that the styles of African-American boys are accommodated.

I would like to share with you an example of a student's ability being misread as a result of a mismatch between the student's and teacher's cultural use of language. Second-grader Marti was reading a story she had written that began, "Once upon a time, there was an old lady, and this old lady ain't had no sense." The teacher interrupted her, "Marti, that sounds like the beginning of a wonderful story, but could you tell me how you would say it in Standard English?" Marti put her head down, thought for a minute, and said softly, "There was an old lady who didn't have any sense." Then Marti put her hand on her hip, raised her voice and said, "But this old lady ain't had *no* sense!" Marti's teacher probably did not understand that the child was actually exhibiting a very sophisticated sense of language. Although she clearly knew the Standard English form, she chose a so-called nonstandard form for emphasis, just as world-class writers Charles Chesnutt, Alice Walker, Paul Lawrence Dunbar, and Zora Neale Hurston have done for years. Of course, there is no standardized test presently on the market that can discern that level of sophistication. Marti's misuse of

Standard English would simply be assessed as a "mistake." Thus, differences in cultural language patterns make inappropriate assessments commonplace.

Another example of assessment difficulties arising from differences in culture can be found in the Latino community. Frequently, Latino girls find it difficult to speak out or exhibit academic prowess in a gender-mixed setting. They will often defer to boys, displaying their knowledge only when in the company of other girls. Most teachers, unaware of this tendency, are likely to insist that all groups be gender-mixed, thus depressing the exhibition of ability by the Latino girls in the class.

A final example involves Native Americans. In many Native American communities there is a prohibition against speaking for someone else. So strong is this prohibition that to the question, "Does your son like moose?," an adult Native American man responded to what should have been asked instead: "*I* like moose." The consequence of this cultural interactional pattern may have contributed to the findings in Charlotte Basham's study of a group of Native American college students' writing. The students appeared unable to write summaries and, even when explicitly told not to, continued to write their opinions of various works rather than summaries of the authors' words. Basham concludes that the prohibition against speaking for others may have caused these students considerable difficulty in trying to capture in their own words the ideas of another. Because they had been taught to always speak for themselves, they found doing so much more comfortable and culturally compatible.

STEREOTYPING

There is a widespread belief that Asian-American children are the "perfect" students, that they will do well regardless of the academic setting in which they are placed. This stereotype has led to a negative backlash in which the academic needs of the majority of Asian-American students are overlooked. I recall one five-year-old Asian-American girl in a Montessori kindergarten class. Cathy was dutifully going about the task assigned to her, that of placing a number of objects next to various numerals printed on a cloth. She appeared to be thoroughly engaged, attending totally to the task at hand, and never disturbing anyone near her. Meanwhile, the teacher's attention was devoted to the children who demanded her presence in one form or another or to those she believed would have difficulty with the task assigned them. Small, quiet Cathy fit neither category. At the end of work time, no one had come to see what Cathy had done, and Cathy neatly put away her work. Her behavior and attention to task had been exemplary. The only problem was that at the end of the session no numeral had the correct number of objects next to it. The teacher later told me that Cathy, like Asian-American students she had taught previously, was one of the best students in the class. Yet, in this case, a child's culturally influenced, nondisruptive classroom behavior, along with the teacher's stereotype of "good Asian students," led to her not receiving appropriate instruction.

Another example of stereotyping involves African-American girls. Research has been conducted in classroom settings which shows that African-American girls are rewarded for nurturing behavior while white girls are rewarded for academic behavior. Though it is likely true that many African-American girls are excellent nurturers, having played with or helped to care for younger siblings or cousins, they are penalized by the nurturing "mammy" stereotype when they are not given the same encouragement as white girls toward academic endeavors.

Another example of stereotyping concerns Native American children. Many researchers and classroom teachers have described the "nonverbal Indian child." What is often missed in these descriptions is that these children are as verbal and eager to share their knowledge as any others, but they need appropriate contexts – such as small groups – in which to talk. When asked inappropriate questions or called on to talk before the entire class, many Native American children will refuse to answer, or will answer in as few words as possible.

Thus, teachers sometimes refrain from calling on Native American students to avoid causing them discomfort, and these children subsequently miss the opportunity to discuss or display their knowledge of the subject matter.

A primary source of stereotyping is often the teacher education program itself. It is in these programs that teachers learn that poor students and students of color should be expected to achieve less than their "mainstream" counterparts.

CHILD-DEFICIT ASSUMPTIONS THAT LEAD TO TEACHING LESS INSTEAD OF MORE

We say we believe that all children can learn, but few of us really believe it. Teacher education usually focuses on research that links failure and socioeconomic status, failure and cultural difference, and failure and single-parent households. It is hard to believe that these children can possibly be successful after their teachers have been so thoroughly exposed to so much negative indoctrination. When teachers receive that kind of education, there is a tendency to assume deficits in students rather than to locate and teach to strengths. To counter this tendency, educators must have knowledge of children's lives outside of school so as to recognize their strengths.

One of my former students is a case in point. Howard was in first grade when everyone thought that he would need to be placed in special education classes. Among his other academic problems, he seemed totally unable to do even the simplest mathematics worksheets. During the unit on money, determining the value of nickels and dimes seemed hopelessly beyond him. I agreed with the general assessment of him until I got to know something about his life outside of school. Howard was seven years old. He had a younger sister who was four and afflicted with cerebral palsy. His mother was suffering from a drug problem and was unable to adequately care for the children, so Howard was the main caretaker in the family. Each morning, he would get his sister up, dressed, and off to school. He also did the family laundry and much of the shopping. To do both those tasks, he had become expert at counting money and knowing when or if the local grocer was overcharging. Still, he was unable to complete what appeared to his teachers to be a simple worksheet. Without teachers having knowledge of his abilities outside of school he was destined to be labeled mentally incompetent.

This story also exposes how curriculum content is typically presented. Children who may be gifted in real-life settings are often at a loss when asked to exhibit knowledge solely through decontextualized paper-and-pencil exercises. I have often pondered that if we taught African-American children how to dance in school, by the time they had finished the first five workbooks on the topic, we would have a generation of remedial dancers!

If we do not have some knowledge of children's lives outside of the realms of paper-and-pencil work, and even outside of their classrooms, then we cannot know their strengths. Not knowing students' strengths leads to our "teaching down" to children from communities that are culturally different from that of the teachers in the school. Because teachers do not want to tax what they believe to be these students' lower abilities, they end up teaching less when, in actuality, these students need *more* of what school has to offer. This is not a new concept. In 1933 Carter G. Woodson discussed the problem in *The Mis-Education of the Negro:*

> The teaching of arithmetic in the fifth grade in a backward county in Mississippi should mean one thing in the Negro school and a decidedly different thing in the white school. The Negro children, as a rule, come from the homes of tenants and peons who have to migrate annually from plantation to plantation, looking for light which they have never seen. The children from the homes of white planters and merchants live permanently in the midst of calculation, family budgets, and the like, which enable them sometimes to learn more by contact than the Negro can acquire in school. Instead of teaching such Negro children less arithmetic, they should be taught much more of it than white children.

Teaching less rather than teaching more can happen in several ways. Those who utilize "skills-based" approaches can teach less by focusing solely on isolated, decontextualized bits. Such instruction becomes boring and meaningless when not placed in any meaningful context. When instruction allows no opportunity for children to use their minds to create and interpret texts, then children will only focus on low-level thinking and their school-based intellect will atrophy. Skills-oriented approaches that feature heavy doses of readiness activities also contribute to the "teaching less" phenomenon. Children are typically assigned to these activities as a result of low scores on some standardized test. However, they end up spending so much time matching circles and triangles that no one ever introduces them to actually learning how to read. Should anyone doubt it, I can guarantee you that no amount of matching circles and triangles ever taught anyone how to read. Worse, these activities take time away from real kinds of involvement in literacy such as listening to and seeing the words in real books.

Teaching less can also occur with those who favor "holistic" or "child-centered" approaches. While I believe that there is much of value in whole language and process writing approaches, some teachers seem almost to be using these methodologies as excuses for not teaching. I am reminded of a colleague who visited a classroom in California designed around the state-mandated whole language approach. My colleague witnessed one child in a peer reading group who clearly could not read. When she later asked the teacher about this child, the teacher responded that it was "OK" that this fourth-grader could not read, because he would understand the content via the subsequent discussion. While it is great that the child would have the opportunity to learn through a discussion, it is devastating that no one was providing him with what he also needed – explicit instruction in learning how to read.

In some "process writing" classrooms, teachers unfamiliar with the language abilities of African-American children are led to believe that these students have no fluency with language. They therefore allow them to remain in the first stages of the writing process, producing first draft after first draft, with no attention to editing or completing final products. They allow African-American students to remain at the level of developing fluency because these teachers do not understand the language competence their students already possess. The key here is not the kind of instruction but the attitude underlying it. When teachers do not understand the potential of the students they teach, they will underteach them no matter what the methodology.

IGNORANCE OF COMMUNITY NORMS

Many school systems have attempted to institute "parent training" programs for poor parents and parents of color. While the intentions of these programs are good, they can only be truly useful when educators understand the realities with which such parents must contend and why they do what they do. Often, middle-class school professionals are appalled by what they see of poor parents, and most do not have the training or the ability to see past surface behaviors to the meanings behind parents' actions.

In a preschool I have often visited, four-year-old David's young mother once came to his class to provide a birthday party for her son. I happened to hear the conversation of the teachers that afternoon. They said she came to school in a "bum costume" yelling, "Let's party!" and running around the room. She had presents for all the children and a cake she or someone else had baked for the occasion. The teachers were horrified. They said they could smell alcohol on her breath, that the children went wild, and that they attempted to get the children out to recess as quickly as possible.

From an earlier conversation, I happened to know that this woman cares deeply for her son and his welfare. She is even saving money to put him in private school — a major sacrifice for her — when he enters kindergarten. David's teachers, however, were not able to see that, despite her possible inappropriateness, his mother had actually spent a great deal of effort and care in putting together this party for her son. She also probably felt the need to bolster her courage a bit with a drink in order to face fifteen four-year-olds and keep them entertained. We must find ways for professionals to understand the different ways in which parents can show their concern for their children.

Another example of a cultural barrier between teacher understandings and parental understandings occurred at a predominantly Latino school in Boston. Even though the teachers continually asked them not to, the parents, primarily mothers, kept bringing their first graders into their classroom before the school day officially began. The teachers wanted all children to remain on the playground with a teacher's aide, and they also wanted all parents to vacate the school yard as soon as possible while the teachers readied the classrooms for the beginning of the day. When the parents continued to ignore the request, the teachers began locking the school doors. Pretty soon feelings escalated to the point of yelling matches, and the parents even approached the school board.

What the teachers in this instance did not understand was that the parents viewed six-year-olds as still being babies and in need of their mother's or their surrogate mother's (the teacher's) attention. To the parents, leaving children outside without one of their "mothers" present was tantamount to child abuse and exhibited a most callous disregard for the children's welfare. The situation did not have to have become so highly charged. All that was needed was some knowledge about the parents and community of the children they were teaching, and the teachers could have resolved the problem easily – perhaps by stationing one of the first-grade teachers outside in the mornings, or by inviting one of the parents to remain on the school grounds before the teachers called the children in to class.

INVISIBILITY

Whether we are immediately aware of it or not, the United States is surely composed of a plethora of perspectives. I am reminded of this every time I think of my friend Martha, a

Native American teacher. Martha told me how tired she got of being asked about her plans for Thanksgiving by people who seemed to take no note that her perspective on the holiday might be a bit different than their own. One year, in her frustration, she told me that when the next questioner asked, "What are you doing for Thanksgiving?", she answered, "I plan to spend the day saying, 'You're welcome!'"

If we plan to survive as a species on this planet we must certainly create multicultural curricula that educate our children to the differing perspectives of our diverse population. In part, the problems we see exhibited in school by African-American children and children of other oppressed minorities can be traced to this lack of a curriculum in which they can find represented the intellectual achievements of people who look like themselves. Were that not the case, these children would not talk about doing well in school as "acting white." Our children of color need to see the brilliance of their legacy, too.

Even with well-intentioned educators, not only our children's legacies but our children themselves can become invisible. Many of the teachers we educate, and indeed their teacher educators, believe that to acknowledge a child's color is to insult him or her. In her book *White Teacher,* Vivian Paley openly discusses the problems inherent in the statement that I have heard many teachers – well-intentioned teachers – utter, "I don't see color, I only see children." What message does this statement send? That there is something wrong with being black or brown, that it should *not* be noticed? I would like to suggest that if one does not see color, then one does not really see children. Children made "invisible" in this manner become hard-pressed to see themselves worthy of notice.

ADDRESSING THE PROBLEMS OF EDUCATING POOR AND CULTURALLY DIVERSE CHILDREN

To begin with, our prospective teachers are exposed to descriptions of failure rather than models of success. We expose student teachers to an education that relies upon name calling and labelling ("disadvantaged," "at-risk," "learning disabled," "the underclass") to explain its failures, and calls upon research study after research study to inform teachers that school achievement is intimately and inevitably linked with socioeconomic status. Teacher candidates are told that "culturally different" children are mismatched to the school setting and therefore cannot be expected to achieve as well as white, middle-class children. They are told that children of poverty are developmentally slower than other children.

Seldom, however, do we make available to our teacher initiates the many success stories about educating poor children and children of color: those institutions like the Nairobi Day-School in East Palo Alto, California, which produced children from poor African-American communities who scored three grade levels above the national average. Nor do we make sure that they learn about those teachers who are quietly going about the job of producing excellence in educating poor and culturally diverse students: teachers like Marva Collins of Chicago, Illinois, who has educated many African-American students considered uneducable by public schools; Jaime Escalante, who has consistently taught hundreds of Latino high school students who live in the poorest *barrios* of East Los Angeles to test their way into advanced-placement calculus classes; and many other successful unsung heroes and heroines who are seldom visible in teacher education classrooms.

Interestingly, even when such teaching comes to our consciousness, it is most often not by way of educational research but via the popular media. We educators do not typically research and document this "power pedagogy" (as Asa Hilliard calls it), but continue to provide, at worst, autopsies of failure and, at best, studies in minimalist achievement. In other words, we teach teachers rationales for failure, not visions of success. Is there any wonder that those who are products of such teacher education (from classroom teachers to principals to central office staff) water down the curriculum for diverse students instead of challenging them with more, as Woodson says, of what school has to offer?

A second reason problems occur for our culturally diverse

students is that we have created in most schools institutions of isolation. We foster the notion that students are clients of "professional" educators who are met in the "office" of the classroom where their deficiencies are remediated and their intellectual "illnesses" healed. Nowhere do we foster inquiry into who our students really are or encourage teachers to develop links to the often rich home lives of students, yet teachers cannot hope to begin to understand who sits before them unless they can connect with the families and communities from which their students come. To do that, it is vital that teachers and teacher educators explore their own beliefs and attitudes about non-white and non-middle-class people. Many teachers – black, white, and "other" – harbor unexamined prejudices about people from ethnic groups or classes different from their own. This is partly because teachers have been so conditioned by the larger society's negative stereotypes of certain ethnic groups, and partly because they are never given the opportunity to learn to value the experiences of other groups.

I propose that a part of teacher education include bringing parents and community members into the university classroom to tell prospective teachers (and their teacher educators) what their concerns about education are, what they feel schools are doing well or poorly for their children, and how they would like to see schooling changed. I would also like to see teacher initiates and their educators go out to community gatherings to acquire such firsthand knowledge. It is unreasonable to expect that teachers will automatically value the knowledge that parents and community members bring to the education of diverse children if valuing such knowledge has not been modelled for them by those from whom they learn to teach.

Following a speech I made at a conference a few years ago, I have been corresponding with a very insightful teacher who works at a prestigious university lab school. The school is staffed by a solely European-American faculty, but seeks to maintain racial and cultural balance among the student body. They find, however, that they continue to lose black students, especially boys. The teacher, named Richard, wrote to me that the school often has problems, both behavioral and academic, with African-American boys. When called to the school to discuss these problems, these children's parents typically say that they do not understand, that their children are fine at home. The school personnel interpret these statements as indications of the parents' "being defensive," and presume that the children are as difficult at home as at school, but that the parents do not want to admit it.

When Richard asked for some suggestions, my first recommendation was that the school should work hard to develop a multicultural staff. Of course, that solution would take a while, even if the school was committed to it. My next and actually most important suggestion was that the school needed to learn to view its African-American parents as a resource and not as a problem. When problems arise with particular African-American children, the school should get the parents of these children involved in helping to point out what the school might do better.

Richard wrote back to me:

> The change though that has made me happiest so far about my own work is that I have taken your advice and I am asking black parents about stuff I never would have brought up before....We do a lot of journal writing, and with the 6- to 8-year-olds I teach, encourage them to draw as well as write, to see the journal as a form of expression. I was having a conference with the mother of one black boy....We looked at his journal and saw that he was doing beautiful intricate drawings, but that he rarely got more than a few words down on the page. I talked to his mother about how we were trying to encourage C. to do the writing first, but that he liked to draw.
>
> During the conversation I started to see this as something like what you were talking about, and I asked C.'s mom how she would handle this at home. I only asked her about how she herself might deal with this, but she said, "In black families, we would just tell him write the words first." I passed that information on to C.'s reading teacher, and we both talked to him and told him he had to get the words down first. Suddenly he began making one- and two-page entries into his journal.
>
> While this is pleasing in and of itself, it is an important lesson to us in terms of equity. C. is now getting equal access to the curricu-

lum because he is using the journal for the reasons we intended it. All we needed was a culturally appropriate way to tell him how to do it.

I am not suggesting that excellent teachers of diverse students *must* be of their students' ethnicity. I have seen too many excellent European-American teachers of African-American students, and too many poor African-American teachers of African-American students to come to such an illogical conclusion. I do believe, however, that we should strive to make our teaching force diverse, for teachers who share the ethnic and cultural backgrounds of our increasingly diverse student bodies may serve, along with parents and other community members, to provide insights that might otherwise remain hidden.

The third problem I believe we must overcome is the narrow and essentially Eurocentric curriculum we provide for our teachers. At the university level, teachers are not being educated with the broad strokes necessary to prepare them properly for the twenty-first century. We who are concerned about teachers and teaching must insist that our teachers become knowledgeable of the liberal arts, but we must also work like the dickens to change liberal arts courses so that they do not continue to reflect only, as feminist scholar Peggy McIntosh says, "the public lives of white Western men." These new courses must not only teach what white Westerners have to say about diverse cultures, they must also share what the writers and thinkers of diverse cultures have to say about themselves, their history, music, art, literature, politics, and so forth.

If we know the intellectual legacies of our students, we will gain insight into how to teach them. Stephanie Terry, a first-grade teacher I have recently interviewed, breathes the heritage of her students into the curriculum. Stephanie teaches in an economically strapped community in inner-city Baltimore, Maryland, in a school with a 100 percent African-American enrollment. She begins each year with the study of Africa, describing Africa's relationship to the United States, its history, resources, and so forth. As her students learn each new aspect of the regular citywide curriculum, Stephanie connects this knowledge to aspects of their African ancestry: while covering a unit about libraries she tells them about the world's first libraries, which were established in Africa. A unit on health presents her with the opportunity to tell her students about the African doctors of antiquity who wrote the first texts on medicine. Stephanie does not replace the current curriculum; rather, she expands it. She also teaches about the contributions of Asian-Americans, Native Americans, and Latinos as she broadens her students' minds and spirits. All of Stephanie's students learn to read by the end of the school year. They also learn to love themselves, love their history, and love learning.

Stephanie could not teach her children the pride of their ancestry and could not connect it to the material they learn today were it not for her extraordinarily broad knowledge of the liberal arts. However, she told me that she did not acquire this knowledge in her formal education, but worked, read, and studied on her own to make such knowledge a part of her pedagogy.

Teachers must not merely take courses that tell them how to treat their students as multicultural clients, in other words, those that tell them how to identify differences in interactional or communicative strategies and remediate appropriately. They must also learn about the brilliance the students bring with them "in their blood." Until they appreciate the wonders of the cultures represented before them – and they cannot do that without extensive study most appropriately begun in college-level courses – they cannot appreciate the potential of those who sit before them, nor can they begin to link their students' histories and worlds to the subject matter they present in the classroom.

If we are to successfully educate all of our children, we must work to remove the blinders built of stereotypes, monocultural instructional methodologies, ignorance, social distance, biased research, and racism. We must work to destroy those blinders so that it is possible to really see, to really know the students we must teach. Yes, if we are to be successful at educating diverse children, we must accomplish the Herculean feat of developing this clear-sightedness, for in the words of a wonderful Native Alaskan educator: "In order to teach you, I must know you." I pray for all of us the strength to teach our children what they must learn, and the humility and wisdom to learn from them so that we might better teach.

Notes

THE SILENCED DIALOGUE

1. See chapter 1 of this volume, "Skills and Other Dilemmas of a Progressive Black Educator."

2. Such a discussion, limited as it is by space constraints, must treat the intersection of class and race somewhat simplistically. For the sake of clarity, however, let me define a few terms: "black" is used herein to refer to those who share some or all aspects of "core black culture" (see John Gwaltney, *Drylongso*, New York: The New Press, 1993), that is, the mainstream of black America – neither those who have entered the ranks of the bourgeoisie nor those who are participants in the disenfranchised underworld. "Middle-class" is used broadly to refer to the predominantly white American "mainstream." There are, of course, nonwhite people who also fit into this category; at issue is their cultural identification, not necessarily the color of their skin. (I must add that there are other nonwhite people, as well as poor white people, who have indicated to me that their perspectives are similar to those attributed herein to black people.)

3. *Multicultural Britain: "Crosstalk,"* National Centre of Industrial Language Training, Commission for Racial Equality, London, England, John Twitchin, producer.

4. See, for example, M.W. Apple, *Ideology and Curriculum* (Boston: Routledge and Kegan Paul, 1979).

5. See E.V. Siddle, "A Critical Assessment of the Natural Process Approach to Teaching Writing," unpublished qualifying paper, Harvard University, 1986.

6. See E.V. Siddle, "The Effect of Intervention Strategies on the Revisions Ninth Graders Make in a Narrative Essay," unpublished doctoral dissertation, Harvard University, 1988.

7. Shirley Brice Heath, *Ways with Words* (Cambridge, Eng.: Cambridge University Press, 1983), p. 280.

8. C. E. Snow, A. Arlman-Rup, Y. Hassing, J. Josbe, J. Joosten, and J. Vorster, "Mother's Speech in Three Social Classes," *Journal of Psycholinguistic Research* 5 (1976), pp. 1–20.

9. Heath, *Ways with Words,* p. 280.

10. I would like to thank Michelle Foster, who is presently planning a more in-depth treatment of the subject, for her astute clarification of the idea.

11. Michelle Foster, "'It's Cookin Now': An Ethnographic Study of the Teaching Style of a Successful Black Teacher in a White Community College," unpublished doctoral disseration, Harvard University, 1987, pp. 67–68.

12. Ibid., p. 68.

13. B. Bernstein makes a similar point when he proposes that different educational frames cannot be successfully institutionalized in the lower levels of education until there are fundamental changes at the postsecondary levels (see "Class and Pedagogies: Visible and Invisible," in B. Bernstein, *Class, Codes, and Control,* vol. 3 [Boston: Routledge and Kegan Paul, 1975]).

14. J. Britton, T. Burgess, N. Martin, A. McLeod, and H. Rosen, *The Development of Writing Abilities* (London: Macmillan Education for the Schools Council, and Urbana, Ill.: National Council of Teachers of English, 1975/1977), p. 54.

15. Ibid., p. 20.

16. G. C. Massey, M. V. Scott, and S. M. Dornbusch, "Racism without Racists: Institutional Racism in Urban Schools," *The Black Scholar* 7.3 (1975), pp. 2–11.

LANGUAGE DIVERSITY AND LEARNING

1. Stephen D. Drashen, *Principles and Practice in Second Language Acquisition* (New York: Pergamon, 1982).

2. Ibid., p. 22.

3. S. Nelson-Barber, "Phonologic Variations of Pima English," in R. St. Clair and W. Leap, eds., *Language Renewal among American Indian Tribes: Issues, Problems and Prospects* (Rosslyn, Va.: National Clearinghouse for Bilingual Education, 1982).

4. Some of these books include Lucille Clifton, *All Us Come 'Cross the Water* (New York: Holt, Rinehart, and Winston, 1973); Paul

Green (aided by Abbe Abbott), *I Am Eskimo – Aknik My Name* (Juneau, Alaska: Alaska Northwest Publishing, 1959); Howard Jacobs and Jim Rice, *Once upon a Bayou* (New Orleans, La.: Phideaux Publications, 1983); Tim Edler, *Santa Cajun's Christmas Adventure* (Baton Rouge, La.: Little Cajun Books, 1981); and a series of biographies produced by Yukon-Koyukkuk School District of Alaska and published by Hancock House Publishers in North Vancouver, British Columbia, Canada.

5. Shirley Brice Heath, *Ways with Words* (Cambridge, Eng.: Cambridge University Press, 1983).

6. S. Michaels and C. B. Cazden, "Teacher-Child Collaboration on Oral Preparation for Literacy," in B. Schieffer, ed., *Acquisition of Literacy: Ethnographic Perspectives* (Norwood, N.J.: Ablex, 1986).

7. C. B. Cazden, *Classroom Discourse* (Portsmouth, N.H.: Heinemann, 1988).

8. Ibid., p. 18.

9. Ibid.

10. Heath, *Ways with Words.*

11. H. Mehan, "Asking Known Information," *Theory into Practice* 28 (1979), pp. 285–94.

12. Ibid., p. 124.

13. G. Smitherman, *Talkin and Testifyin* (Boston: Houghton Mifflin, 1977).

14. R. Sims, "Dialect and Reading: Toward Redefining the Issues," in J. Langer and M. T. Smith-Burke, eds., *Reader Meets Author/ Bridging the Gap* (Newark, Dela.: International Reading Association, 1982).

15. Ibid.

16. P. M. Cunningham, "Teachers' Correction Responses to Black-Dialect Miscues Which Are Nonmeaning-Changing," *Reading Research Quarterly* 12 (1976–77).

17. Robert Berdan, "Knowledge into Practice: Delivering Research to Teachers," in M. F. Whiteman, ed., *Reactions to Ann Arbort: Vernacular Black English and Education* (Arlington, Va.: Center for Applied Linguistics, 1980).

18. Ibid., p. 78.

19. R. Kaplan, "Cultural Thought Patterns in Intercultural Education," *Language Learning* 16 (1966), pp. 1–2.

20. Cazden, *Classroom Discourse,* p. 12.

21. Heath, *Ways with Words.*

22. Ron Scollon and Suzanne B. K. Scollon, "Cooking It Up and Boiling It Down: Abstracts in Athabaskan Children's Story Retellings," in D. Tannen, ed., *Spoken and Written Language* (Norwood, N.J.: Ablex, 1979).

23. Eleanor Wilson Orr, *Twice as Less: Black English and the Performance of Black Students in Mathematics and Science* (New York: W.W. Norton, 1987).

24. Ibid., p. 30.

25. Ibid., 149 (emphasis added).

26. Personal communication, 1988.

27. Personal communication, 1989.

THE VILIS TOKPLES SCHOOLS
OF PAPUA NEW GUINEA

1. A. Taylor, "Language Policy in Papua New Guinea," *The Linguistic Reporter* 24.1 (Sept. 1981).

2. D. Laycock, "Pidgin's Progress," in E.B. Thomas, ed., *Papua New Guinea Education* (Melbourne: Oxford University Press, 1976).

3. G. Sankoff, *The Social Life of Language* (Philadelphia: University of Pennsylvania Press, 1980).

4. M. Meggitt, "Uses of Literacy in New Guinea and Melanesia," in J. Goody, ed., *Literacy in Traditional Societies* (Cambridge, Eng.: Cambridge University Press, 1968).

5. G. Smith, *Education in Papua New Guinea* (Melbourne: Melbourne University Press, 1975), p. 11.

6. D. J. Dickson, "Education, History, and Development," part 1, in P. Ryan, ed., *Encyclopaedia of Papua and New Guinea* (Melbourne: Melbourne University Press, 1972).

7. [Papua New Guinea] Department of Education, *Education Plan 1976–1980* (Port Moresby, Papua New Guinea: Department of Education, 1976).

8. D. F. Lancy, ed., *Papua New Guinea Journal of Education* 15, special issue: *The Community School* (1979).

9. Lisa Delpit, *Language, Culture, and Self-determination: An Ethnographically Based Evaluation of an Experiment in Schooling in Papua New Guinea,* doctoral dissertation, Harvard University, 1984.

10. G. Kemelfield, "Upe: The Getting of Wisdom in the North Solomons," in G. Guthrie and P. Smith, eds., *The Education of the Papua New Guinea Child* (Port Moresby: University of Papua New Guinea, 1980.); and Smith, *Education in Papua New Guinea.*

11. A Kituai, "Education Has Robbed Me of My Child," paper presented at a History Department seminar, University of Papua New Guinea, 1976.

12. Quoted in B. Cheetham, "School and Community in the Huli Area of the Southern Highlands Province," *Papua New Guinea Journal of Education* 15, special issue: *The Community School* (1979).

13. R. Kovoho, *Teacher Training for Viles Tok Ples Skul Scheme in the North Solomons Province,* ERU Report 51, (Port Moresby, Papua New Guinea: Educational Research Unit, University of Papua New Guinea, 1985).

14. Kemelfield, "Upe."

15. B. Anderson, ed., *The Right to Learn: The Neglect of Non-formal Education* (Port Moresby, Papua New Guinea: Department of Education, University of Papua New Guinea, 1981).

16. J. Allen and C. Hurd, *Languages of the Bougainville District* (Papua New Guinea: Summer Institute of Linguistics, 1963).

17. As part of the research study, I tested children in Buka and Buin, and found that although they had not been taught formally in Tok Pisin, they were able to read and write the language as a result of having become literate in their *tok ples.*

18. J. A. Fishman, *Bilingual Education: An International Sociological Perspective* (Rowley, Mass.: Newbury House, 1976), p. 73.

HELLO, GRANDFATHER

1. Ron and Suzanne B. K. Scollon, *Narrative, Literacy, and Face in Interethnic Communication* (Norwood, N.J.: Ablex, 1981).

2. John Gwaltney, *Drylongso* (New York: The New Press, 1993), p. 22.

TEACHERS' VOICES

1. Notable among many articles are the following: J.C. Baratz, "Black Participation in the Teacher Pool," paper prepared for the Carnegie Forum's Task Force on Teaching as a Profession, November, 1986; B. Bass de Martinez, "Political and Reform

Agendas' Impact on the Supply of Black Teachers," *Journal of Teacher Education* 39.1 (1988); P. A.Garcia, "The Impact of National Testing on Ethnic Minorities: With Proposed Solutions," *Journal of Negro Education* 55.3 (1986); A. M. Garibaldi, *The Decline of Teacher Production in Louisiana (1976–83) and Attitudes Toward the Profession* (Atlanta: Southern Education Foundation, 1986); G. Sykes, "The Social Consequences of Standard Setting in the Professions," paper prepared for the Carnegie Forum's Task Force on Teaching as a Profession, November 1986; and B. Taylor, "Generating Reform in the Teaching Profession: What Are the Implications of the Holmes and Carnegie Reports for Black Educators and Black Children?", *Perspective,* Newsletter of the American Educational Research Association's special interest group, Research Focus on Black Education (Spring 1986).

2. P. A.Graham, "Black Teachers: A Drastically Scarce Resource," *The Kappan* 68.8 (1987).

3. D. Kauffman, "Wingspread Conference: Consensus Reached on Policy about Minorities in Teaching," *Briefs* 8.7 (1987).

4. Graham, "Black Teachers," p. 599.

5. The interviewees were six Native Americans and six African-Americans, eleven women and one man, ranging in age from 32–73, who completed teacher education programs between 1952 and 1987. As of this writing, three had never entered the teaching force; one other left after two years of teaching; two taught for several years and then became principals; one is presently in an administrative position but hopes to return to the classroom; one is on leave from a teaching position in order to pursue a graduate degree; three are presently classroom teachers; and one is retired. The interviews were taped, usually in the interviewer's or the interviewee's home. There was no attempt to seek a random sample, as these interviews are a part of ongoing research that aims to interview all of the teachers of color in Fairbanks (a total of about forty individuals). Fairbanks is a predominantly white town of about eighty-five thousand.

   The meeting with Native teachers was held in a rural Athabaskan village. Six teachers and this researcher were in attendance. The telephone calls to black teachers served primarily to help validate the findings from the interviews.

6. Shirley Brice Heath, *Ways with Words.* (Cambridge, Eng.: Cambridge University Press, 1983); T. Kochman, *Black and White Styles in Conflict* (Chicago: University of Chicago Press, 1981); Ron Scollon and Suzanne B.K. Scollon, *Narrative, Literacy, and Face in Interethnic Communication* (Norwood, N.J.: Ablex, 1981);

Smitherman, *Talkin and Testifyin* (Boston: Houghton Mifflin, 1977).

7. D. Hymes with C. Cazden, "Narrative Thinking and Story-telling Rights: A Folklorist's Clue to a Critique of Education," in D. Hymes, *Language in Education: Ethnolinguistic Essays* (Washington, D.C.: Center for Applied Linguistics, 1980).

8. Regarding this point, see Scollon and Scollon, *Narrative, Literacy, and Face in Interethnic Communication;* and N. Wolfson, "A Feature of Performed Narratives: The Conversational Historical Present," *Language in Society* 7 (1978).

9. Hymes with Cazden, "Narrative Thinking and Storytelling Rights."

10. Because I had not found references in the literature to teachers' feelings of bias in the teacher education program, I was somewhat surprised at the intensity of these feelings expressed in the interviews. It may be that because the interviewer was herself black, and that care was taken to provide a comfortable, conversational setting, teachers felt free to talk about topics they might not otherwise have discussed.

11. N. Benokraitis and J.R. Feagin, *Modern Sexism: Blatant Sexism, Subtle, and Covert Discrimination* (Englewood Cliffs, N.J.: Prentice Hall, 1986).

12. A. Mehrabian, "Relationship of Attitudes to Seated Posture, Orientation and Distance," *Social Psychology* 30 (1968).

13. See, for example, Garibaldi, *The Decline of Teacher Production,* and L. Darling-Hammond, K.J. Pittman, and K. Ottinger, "Career Choices for Minorities: Who Will Teach?", paper prepared for the National Education Association and Council of Chief State School Officers' Task Force on Minorities in Teaching, June 1987.

14. H. Schuman, C. Steeh, and L. Bobo, *Racial Attitudes in America: Trends and Interpretations* (Cambridge, Mass.: Harvard University Press, 1985).

15. T.G. Pettigrew and J. Martin, "Shaping the Organizational Context for Black American Inclusion," *Journal of Social Issues* 43.1 (1987).

16. F. Crosby, S. Bromley, and L. Saxe, "Recent Unobtrusive Studies of Black and White Discrimination and Prejudice: A Literature Review," *Psychological Bulletin* 87 (1980); E. Donnerstein and M. Donnerstein, "Variables in Interracial Aggression: Potential in Group Censure," *Journal of Personality and Social Psychology* 27

(1973); Pettigrew and Martin, "Shaping the Organizational Context"; S. Weitz, "Attitude, Voice, and Behavior: A Repressed Affect Model of Interracial Interaction," *Journal of Personality and Social Psychology* 24 (1972), pp. 14–21; L. Wispé and H. Freshly, "Race, Sex, and the Sympathetic Helping Behavior: The Broken Bag Caper," *Journal of Personality and Social Psychology* 17 (1971), pp. 59–65.

17. Pettigrew and Martin, "Shaping the Organizational Context," p. 50.

18. D. E. Berlew and D. T. Hall, "Socialization of Managers: Effects of Expectations on Performance," in D. A. Kolb, I. M. Rubin, and J. M. McIntyre, eds., *Organizational Psychology: A Book of Readings* (3d ed., Englewood Cliffs, N.J.: Prentice Hall, 1971), and C. O. Word, M. P. Zanna, and J. Cooper, "The Nonverbal Mediation of Self-Fulfilling Prophecies in Interracial Interaction," *Journal of Experimental Social Psychology* 10 (1974).

19. G. Griffin, Clinical Preservice Teacher Education: Final Report of a Descriptive Study, Report no. 9026 (Austin: R&D Center for Teacher Education, University of Texas at Austin, 1983), and S. Hollingsworth, *Learning to Teach Reading*, doctoral dissertation, University of Texas at Austin, 1986.

20. S. Merriam, "Mentors and Protégés: A Critical Review of the Literature," *Adult Education Quarterly* 33 (1983).

21. G. B. Northcroft, *Affirmative Action: The Impact of Legislated Equality*, unpublished doctoral dissertation, Stanford University, 1982.

22. Pettigrew and Martin, "Shaping the Organizational Context."

23. John Dewey, "The Relation of Theory to Practice in Education" (1904), in M. L. Borrowman, ed., *Teacher Education in America: A Documentary History* (New York: Teachers College Press, 1965), p. 153.

24. It is possible that these minority teachers are not representative of younger graduates. Some of the interviewees expressed alarm at the possibility that younger people of color were emerging from teacher education with ideas very similar to those of white teachers.

25. I thank Dr. John Tippeconic for his insightful comment cautioning us to beware that the student of color not be viewed as an expert only on issues regarding ethnicity. It is the instructor's role to ensure that these students be heard on other issues as well.

26. Pettigrew and Martin, "Shaping the Organizational Context."

27. E.G. Cohen, "Expectation States and Interracial Interaction in School Settings," *Annual Review of Sociology* 8 (1982), and *Designing Groupwork: Strategies for the Heterogeneous Classroom* (New York: Teachers College Press, 1986); E. Aronson, J. Sikes, N. Blaney, and M. Snapp, *The Jigsaw Classroom* (Beverly Hills, Calif.: Sage, 1978).

INTERVIEW SCHEDULE

1. What is your present job? What makes it good? What makes it difficult?

2. Do you think your ideas about teaching are different from other educators around you? How so?

3. What made you decide to become a teacher?

4. What kind of place did you do your teacher training in? Was that a good experience? [Graduate education?]

5. Did you feel that what you were taught was relevant to you and the children you wanted to teach? [Graduate education?]

6. What do you think has influenced your teaching most? Did you have any role models that influenced your teaching?

7. What did you learn in teacher training that is useful to you now?

8. Were you taught anything you thought was just wrong?

9. What was the relationship between you and non-minority faculty and students?

10. What would have made your teacher training experience better? Different faculty? Different curriculum? Different structure?

LOOKING TO THE FUTURE: ACCOMMODATING DIVERSITY

1. "Acquisition of Literate Discourse: Bowing Before the Master?", *Theory into Practice* vol. XXXI, No. 4 special issue, Vivian Gadsden, ed.: (1992).

2. James Fraser and Theresa Perry, eds., *Freedom's Plow* (New York: Routledge, 1993).

3. Glauber, Bill, "A Community Fractured: Resentments Fester in Alabama Town Jolted by School Arson," *The Baltimore Sun,* August 14, 1994.

CROSS-CULTURAL CONFUSIONS
IN TEACHER ASSESSMENT

1. Jay Featherstone, Comments at the North Dakota Study Group Annual Meeting, February, 1988.

2. Lee Shulman and G. Sykes, "A National Board for Teaching?: In Search of a Bold Standard," paper prepared for the Carnegie Forum on Education and the Economy's Task Force on Teaching as a Profession (1986).

3. But a few of the scholars who have written on the topic are: Shirley Brice Heath, *Ways with Words* (Cambridge, Eng.: Cambridge University Press, 1983); T. Kochman, *Black and White Styles in Conflict* (Chicago: University of Chicago Press, 1981); Smitherman, *Talkin and Testifyin* (Boston: Houghton Mifflin, 1977).

4. Heath, *Ways with Words;* Kochman, *Black and White Styles;* Walter Ong, *Orality and Literacy* (London: Methuen, 1982); Ron Scollon and Suzanne B. K.Scollon, *Narrative, Literacy, and Face in Interethnic Communication* (Norwood, N.J.: Ablex, 1981).

5. Lee Shulman, "Knowledge and Teaching: Foundations of the New Reform," *Harvard Educational Review* 57.1 (1987), p. 7.

6. A. Meek, "On Creating 'Ganas': A Conversation with Jaime Escalante," *Educational Leadership* 46.5 (1989), p. 46.

7. B. Holliday, "Toward a Model of Teacher-Child Transactional Processes Affecting Black Children's Academic Achievement," in M. B. Spencer, G. K. Brookins, and W. R. Allen, eds., *Beginnings: The Social and Affective Development of Black Children* (Hillsdale, N. J.: Lawrence Erlbaum & Assoc., 1985).

8. Barbara Shade, "Ecological Correlates of Educative Style of Afro-American Children," *Journal of Negro Education* 60 (1987), pp. 60, 291–301.

9. Kochman, *Black and White Styles.*

10. D. Duke and A. Mechkel, *Teachers' Guide to Classroom Management* (New York: Random House, 1984)

11. Michelle Foster, "'It's Cookin Now': An Ethnographic Study of the Teaching Style of a Successful Black Teacher in a White Community College," unpublished doctoral dissertation, Harvard University, 1987.

12. See chapter 2 of this volume, and Foster, "'It's Cookin Now'."

13. B. Bernstein, "Social Class, Language, and Socialization," in G. Giglioli, ed., *Language and Social Context* (New York: Penguin,

1972), pp. 157–78; D. Olson, "From Utterance to Text: The Bias of Language in Speech and Writing," *Harvard Educational Review* 47 (1977), pp. 527–81; Ong, *Orality and Literacy.*

14. S. Nelson-Barber and T. Meier, "Bridges to Knowledge: Accounting for 'Cultural Context' in Teacher Education," in *Academic Connections* (New York: The College Board, Office of Academic Affairs, forthcoming); D. Tannen, "Spoken/Written Language and the Oral/Literate Continuum," *Proceedings of the Sixth Annual Meeting of the Berkeley Linguistic Group* (Berkeley, Calif., 1980), pp. 207–18.

15. J. Condon and F. Yousef, *An Introduction to Intercultural Communication* (Indianapolis: Bobbs-Merrill, 1975); B. Goldstein and K. Tamura, *Japan and America: A Comparative Study in Language and Culture* (Rutland, Vt.: Charles E. Tuttle, 1975); Nelson-Barber and Meier, "Bridges to Knowledge"; and Scollon and Scollon, *Narrative, Literacy, and Face in Interethnic Communication.*

16. A. Yan, "Discourse Analysis in Cross-cultural Perspective: A Comparative Study of Japanese and American Students' Public Speeches," paper prepared for the course "Language, Literacy, and Learning," University of Alaska, Fairbanks.

17. Heath, *Ways with Words;* Kochman, *Black and White Styles;* S. Michaels, "Narrative Presentations: An Oral Preparation of Literacy with First Graders," in J. Cook-Gumperz, ed., *The Social Construction of Literacy* (New York: Cambridge University Press, 1986), pp. 94–116; C. Mitchell-Kerman, "Signifying and Marking: Two Afro-American Speech acts," in J. Gumperz and D. Hymes, eds., *Directions in Sociolinguistics: The Ethnography of Communication* (New York: Holt, Rinehart, and Winston, 1972), pp. 161–79; Smitherman, *Talkin and Testifyin.*

18. K. Basso, *Portraits of the Whiteman: Linguistic Play and Cultural Symbols among the Western Apache* (New York: Cambridge University Press, 1979); R. Darnell, "Reflections on Cree Interactional Etiquette: Educational Implications," Sociolinguistic Working Paper no. 57 (Southwest Educational Development Laboratory, 1979); Ina Siler and Diana Labidie-Wondergem, "Cultural Factors in the Organization of Speeches by Native Americans," in F. Barkin, E. Brandt; and J. Ornstein-Galacia, *Bilingualism and Language Contact* (New York: Teachers College Press, 1982), pp. 93–100.

19. Nelson-Barber and Meier, "Bridges to Knowledge"; and Scollon and Scollon, *Narrative, Literacy, and Face in Interethnic Communication.*

20. Scollon and Scollon, *Narrative, Literacy, and Face in Interethnic Communication.*

21. L. Shulman, S. Nelson-Barber, S. Aburto, and J. Mitchell, *Teaching a Familiar Lesson (Mathemathics and History),* Teacher Assessment Project Technical Report No. M10 & H8 (Stanford: Stanford University), pp. 77–78.

22. Ibid., pp. 77–78.

23. Tannen, "Spoken/Written Language."

24. Basso, *Portraits of the Whiteman;* Condon and Yousef, *Introduction to Intercultural Communication;* Goldstein and Tamura, *Japan and America;* Scollon and Scollon, *Narrative, Literacy, and Face in Interethnic Communication.*

THE POLITICS OF TEACHING
LITERATE DISCOURSE

1. *Journal of Education,* special issue: *Literacy, Discourse, and Linguistics: Essays by James Paul Gee* 171.1 (1989).

2. Mike Rose, *Lives on the Boundary* (New York: Free Press, 1989).

3. Anthony M. Platt, *E. Franklin Frazier Reconsidered* (New Brunswick, N.J.: Rutgers University Press, 1991), p. 15.

4. Keith Gilyard, *Voices of the Self* (Detroit: Wayne State University Press, 1991), p. 160.

5. Herbert Kohl, *I Won't Learn from You! The Role of Assent in Education* (Minneapolis, Minn.: Milkweed Editions, 1991).

6. Gee's position here is somewhat different. He argues that grammar and form should be taught in classrooms, but that students will never acquire them with sufficient fluency to gain entry into dominant discourses. Rather, he states, such teaching is important because it allows students to gain "meta-knowledge" of how language works, which in turn "leads to the ability to manipulate, to analyze, to resist while advancing" (*Journal of Education,* special issue 171.1, p. 13).

7. bell hooks, *Talking Back* (Boston: South End Press, 1989), p. 11.

8. See, for example, Carlos Yorio, "The Other Side of the Looking Glass," *Journal of Basic Writing* 8.1 (1989).

9. Henry Louis Gates, Jr., quoted in Reginald Martin, "Black Writer as Black Critic: Recent Afro-American Writing," *College English* 52.2 (Feb. 1990), p. 204.

10. hooks, *Talking Back.*, p. 50.

11. June Jordan, "Nobody Mean More to Me Than You and the Future Life of Willie Jordan," *Harvard Educational Review* 58.3 (1988).

12. hooks, *Talking Back*; and Henry Louis Gates, Jr., *Race, Writing, and Difference* (Chicago: University of Chicago Press, 1986).

13. James D. Anderson, *The Education of Blacks in the South, 1860–1935* (Chapel Hill, N.C.: University of North Carolina Press, 1988), p. 30.

Index

Please remember that this is a library book,
and that it belongs only temporarily to each
person who uses it. Be considerate. Do
not write in this, or any, library book.

Date Due